DAUGHTERHOOD

a memoir

Emily Adrian

autofocus books
Orlando, Florida

Published by Autofocus Books
autofocuslit.com

1st printing

Memoir
ISBN: 978-1-957392-32-5

Cover Illustration ©Amy Wheaton
Library of Congress Control Number: 2024933971

DAUGHTERHOOD

a memoir

Why was I screaming at Wes? He was two and unwilling to get ready for bed. He was two, sobbing and kicking me in the stomach as I wrestled him into pajamas. Really, I was screaming because my husband was sick with a disease we didn't yet know was Rocky Mountain Spotted Fever. If our son had a reason for his nonverbal rebellion, it was that his dad had been to the Emergency Room three times that summer; Dan had stopped offering shoulder rides beneath the hot Virginia sun. He had skipped bedtime stories and mornings at the pool in our building's parking lot. Confused, Wes had regressed and would not let me set him down. It was like having a newborn again except the newborn was thirty-five pounds and never napped.

As I begged him to stop crying, my voice splintered. I felt your hand on my back.

Had I forgotten you were there? Sort of. Two nights ago I had called 911 when Dan couldn't breathe, and then I had called you. You came promptly, as if from across town rather than the opposite coast, though it meant asking your boss forgiveness and not permission. You packed your three favorite shirts, best jeans, hairdryer, reading glasses, and walking shoes.

"What can I do?" you asked now. "Do you want me to take the dog out? Wash the dishes?"

I stiffened. Not with resentment or annoyance, but with

shame. More shame than I knew what to do with. Shame that wasn't going anywhere soon.

*

That was August 2019. By the end of the summer Dan would have a diagnosis, antibiotics, and, for the first time in his life, an understanding of what I meant when I talked about anxiety. You stayed in Richmond about a week. Before you flew back to the West Coast, we left Wes and Dan asleep in the apartment and walked around the corner to the nearest restaurant. Since Wes's birth two years earlier, you and I had rarely been alone together.

You asked me to order you a cocktail—"nothing too sweet." I was nervous and ordered you a drink at random. You took a sip and cringed.

"I want to ask you something," I said.

You steeled yourself. "Okay."

"I want to write a book about your life."

You took a second sip of the sugary cocktail. "I do think you had an interesting childhood."

"Not my life," I said. "Yours. I want to focus on the part after you left home and before you became a mom."

"That was the hardest part," you said, not quite looking at me.

I knew that. But for me, the hardest part was now. I wanted to know why motherhood had saved you, and why it was wrecking me.

*

And then I waited too long to write this book. I was scared. 2019 became 2020, and now I can't interview you in person the way I planned. If I want to learn about your life, I will have to ask you through a screen. Strangely, you and I have never talked much when we're apart. Probably because it makes us sad.

Do you know where I am when I close my eyes? I'm in the front seat of your car. You're trying to tell me a story I'm only half willing to hear. Through the window the Pacific churns against sea stacks, or pine trees brace themselves against a red-dirt canyon. On the radio: Jackson Browne, James Taylor. Songs that take you back to the seventies. Songs Dad never liked because they weren't jazz. I haven't lived out West since I was twenty, but lately I have reverted to saying "home" and meaning Oregon.

Lately, I want the West the way a child wants her mother.

1974

Ellen drives to North's Chuck Wagon for her 5 p.m. shift, though she could have walked. The October afternoon has already faded into the neon glow of McLoughlin Boulevard, where signs for diners and gas stations loom over four lanes of traffic. In the kitchen she ties an apron over her uniform. The brown dress, with its wide collar and pleated skirt, is meant to be hideous. Ellen is young and beautiful in spite of the uniform; her youth and beauty are nonnegotiable.

"You married?" asks her first customer, who has paid a dollar-fifty to load up his plate with prime rib, potatoes specked with parsley, hot apple pie. Old men are always asking her this. They love to hear her say no.

"No." She pours coffee into his mug. Above the cushioned booth hang desert landscapes and a taxidermy jackrabbit.

"Boyfriend?"

"Yes." Sam is new and the best one yet. A non-Mormon. His looks are tidy and symmetrical. A coworker introduced them.

"Your boyfriend want to marry you?"

Her smile is for herself, but she knows how it looks. "I'm sure he does."

The man nods, his expression obscured by a reddish mustache. Before she can move to the next booth, he points at her nametag. "I knew you looked familiar. You're one of Earl's kids."

She lets her posture go slack, childlike. "You know my dad?"

"Used to. We went hunting a few years back."

She doesn't want to tell him about Earl Sr.'s heart attack. Doesn't want to invoke the house from which she, at sixteen, has already moved away.

"When you get home tonight, tell him Larry says hello. Tell him I hope he's feeling better these days."

Home is now the Whispering Pines Trailer Park. Her parents have given her the red trailer formerly occupied by her oldest brother and his teenage bride—but there's a catch. After she graduates high school in the spring, a full year early, she has promised to go to a Mormon college.

"Sure thing," she says, holding the carafe near her right hip. "Need anything else?" She's eager to get to her next table, to be anonymous again. She hates to be remembered as one of seven honey-haired children following their devout mother and Jack Mormon father into church.

His eyes sweep her body. The man wears a blue flannel coat with a textured collar. "You tell your boyfriend he's a lucky man."

*

By the nineties, North's Chuck Wagon had closed. In its place stood a strip club called The Dolphin. A towering blue sign buzzed with a pink promise of GIRLS GIRLS GIRLS. In the parking lot, a plastic pod of dolphins leapt from a pool of dingy water.

We would drive by The Dolphin on our way to the Oak Grove movie theater or Lani Louie's (where the owner still liked to croon your maiden name). Dad would deadpan, "That's where Ellen worked in high school."

Swatting him on the shoulder, you would clarify, "It wasn't a strip club then. It was North's Chuck Wagon, okay? I worked there with my friend Kerry and we raked in the tips like you wouldn't believe."

"Sure sounds like a strip club," he would say.

Either I remember this routine because it was repeated often or because this detail from your past intrigued me. Generally, the kitschy sprawl of the boulevard made my eyes glaze over in Sunday afternoon apathy. But when we passed The Dolphin, I relaxed into an image of you as a teenager. Your broad smile and blonde waves. Your funny homemade clothes.

As a child, what did I know of your childhood? Only flashes, like a movie I'd watched home sick from school. I knew you were thirteen years old when your last two siblings were born: twins, including your only sister. I could not list all five of your brothers, though I recognized their names when you mentioned them. The oldest two were the reason nine of your teeth had been chipped and knocked out of alignment. The reason you'd hidden pets in your closet and dreaded your parents' weekends away.

The list of things you hadn't told me was long.

*

In 2004, I sat in the passenger seat of your Volkswagen Beetle; we were waiting for a light on the same boulevard. At fifteen, restlessness was my identity. I was bored of high school, of supermarkets, of inclement winters and dry, dreamy summers. I was so sick of adolescence, and so unselfconscious in front of you, I didn't think twice about saying, "I hope I'm not still sitting at this intersection when I'm thirty. I hope by then I can say I haven't driven down this street in years."

Behind the steering wheel, you made the face you still make when I hurt your feelings: eyes hard and averted, lips almost smirking.

Would you believe I have never, in my life, meant to hurt your feelings? I have only expected you to absorb my feelings like a sponge.

Initially, I pitched a road trip, the kind we took often when I was growing up. I thought we would drive from Portland to Burns, through Rexburg and Salt Lake City, to Provo and back home. In each of these places I would interview you about your life.

"She's not going to turn you down," Dan said, knowing how you feel about road trips, and me. "Doesn't mean she wants you to write a book about her life."

"She does," I assured him, because you'd said yes. Truthfully, I have approached this project like a child: it doesn't matter to me what you want. It only matters what you'll let me get away with.

I was going to interview you in motel rooms and cabins, across campfires and beneath the mountain ranges of Oregon, Idaho, and Utah. Instead, we meet on Zoom after I've put Wes to bed. The recordings capture the crickets outside my bedroom window in New Haven, Connecticut—my third state in three years. I haven't seen you since February 2020; it is now September.

Even if I could get to Portland, we couldn't drive anywhere. Wildfires have ravaged the West Coast, burning neighborhoods to the ground, turning the sky an extraterrestrial orange. You wake up to your windshield coated in ash. On the evacuation map, our hometown is listed as Level 1: Be ready to leave.

Still, I'm writing a book about your life. Yours instead of mine.

1975

From the backseat, she tells her parents she's sick. Outside the car the cliffs of the Columbia River Gorge loom red and untouchable. "Just try to close your eyes," LaVerne murmurs. She keeps a pliable copy of *The Book of Mormon* in the glove compartment. She sucks on a succession of hard candies as they drive. "You'll feel better after a little rest." Ellen finally sleeps somewhere past Pendleton, her dreams chaotic and abstract. Hours later she wakes to a view of silos and painted barns rising from the tawny, gnarled prairie. She steers her thoughts toward Sam.

Certain memories almost help. The Deep Purple concert at Memorial Coliseum; Sam in a denim shirt bobbing his head to "Smoke on the Water." Or the morning they skipped school, drove to the coast, and ordered fried clams from a gas station on the 101. Wind whipped her hair into her tartar sauce. All last year, Sam worked at Hopp's Upholstery and Shoe Repair in downtown Oregon City. When she could, Ellen drove to the store after school and helped him close. Some nights the Hopps invited the two of them over for dinner. At the Hopps' kitchen table, among their lightly squabbling children, Ellen thought of the blessing she'd received at age thirteen. An elderly patriarch had put his cold hands on her head and held her in place. With the breathlessness of a vacuum salesman, he predicted her future. She would serve her husband's priesthood powers. She would raise her babies righteous in the gospel.

She would preside over a crowded table.

Sam isn't like the boys she dated when she was younger, or the boys to whom she's related. He can't take a car apart and put it back together. He doesn't hunt. He isn't arrogant. And yet Ellen's second oldest brother, Earl Jr., had no trouble convincing Sam to join the Air Force. As she drives to Idaho with her parents—her boyfriend's record player and speakers packed safely in the trunk—Sam makes his way south to the base in Tucson. The sound system was not a gift, but a loan, which Ellen has decided is a form of collateral. Would he give her his record player if he meant never to see her again?

An hour past Twin Falls, Ellen asks her dad to stop the car; she stumbles from the backseat and vomits into the sagebrush beside the highway. The sky is a gray dome. In the hazy distance looms the ridge of a mountain range she can't name. Seven hundred miles feels farther from home than she expected, but the miles make no difference; her parents are her parents, perpetually unconcerned.

At dusk, they pull into the parking lot of a women's dormitory at Ricks College. The building is two stories, with a beige brick facade and a motel's exterior staircase. Her parents take stock of the cinderblock walls, the flimsy kitchen cabinets, the living room's brown carpet.

"You'll be fine here," LaVerne says, with a smile of denial or indifference. Then they leave.

Ellen is seventeen, and she's the first of her five roommates to arrive at the apartment. For the better part of a week, she stays curled across a bottom bunk, sweating into the sheets she brought from home, rising only to use the bathroom or refill a cup with cloudy tap water. The morning her fever breaks, she carries a thick course catalog into bed. On the front cover, two women in long skirts stroll down a paved path. Behind them, a sprinkler douses the lawn.

Her illness is demoralizing, disorienting—but also, isn't there something weird about these course offerings? *Achieving Success in Marriage. Synchronized Swimming. The Doctrine and Covenants. Trampoline & Tumbling. The Gospel in Principle and Practice. Ra-*

cial and Minority Group Relations. Rodeo. None of the course descriptions conjures the scholarly, sun-dappled college experience Ellen has read about, seen in movies. The section titled *Standards: Conduct, Dress, and Grooming* goes on longer than the schedule of English classes. Boys can wear jeans; girls cannot.

*

You helped me move into my first apartment, a studio on SW 12th Avenue in Portland. You gave me the yellow armchair from your living room; you bought me a ten-dollar microwave. You showed me how to bleach the stains from the hundred-year-old clawfoot tub.

Since then, I've moved often, between two countries and a handful of states. In 2018 you flew to Ohio to look after Wes while Dan and I loaded a U-Haul. Dan drove the truck straight to Richmond, where he was about to begin his second teaching job. With me, the baby, and the dog as your passengers, you drove our temperamental Mazda across Ohio, through a rainstorm outside Pittsburgh, and into the hills of West Virginia where we'd rented a cabin for two nights.

In West Virginia I was tired. I was tired from the stress and logistics of moving, but I was also tired in a way that was persistently postpartum. Wes had been weaned, and he mostly slept through the night, but motherhood was still a foreign country, one from which I knew I could never return. Fifteen months in, and I didn't understand why I wasn't the kind of mother to Wes that you had been, still were, to me. At my best, I felt like a weak imitation of you, crouching at his side and ineffectively coaching him through his frustration. At my worst, I was still the child tantrumming on the kitchen floor, only now there were two of me.

I couldn't stop snapping at you. Because you'd lived in Oregon so long you'd forgotten how to pump gas. Because the volume at which you did the dishes woke the baby. For lunch we ate tuna fish sandwiches—one of several foods on which, you taught me, a person could survive if she had to. Afterward I disappeared into the dark, mildewed bedroom I was sharing with Wes. I meant to use the bathroom. Instead, I collapsed across the twin mattress. The bedsprings groaned; I fell asleep.

I woke up two hours later, initially unsure if it was the same day or a new one. If I lived in Oregon or Canada or rural Ohio. If I was ten or seventeen or thirty. I found you and Wes among the trees behind the cabin, pushing on an old hammock. In spite of Wes's inability to talk or hold still, you two were angled toward each other as if deep in conversation.

I apologized for falling asleep. You smiled at me.

"What have you been doing?" I asked.

You shrugged. "Just this."

1975

In the apartment she shares with five other girls, Ellen boils water for ramen noodles. Because her parents declined to sign her up for a meal plan, she's been living on the tips she saved waitressing last year. Now the bottom of the saucepan is black from frequent use. Her tongue has become desensitized to the onslaught of salt. She's always a little bit hungry.

After dinner, she zips a bulky, plum-colored parka to her throat and crosses the housing complex to the student lounge, contracting her shoulders against the cold. Girls are piled on a threadbare couch watching a rerun of *M*A*S*H*. Ellen hovers at a distance, waiting for her chance to use the phone. She's seen this one before: nurses evacuated due to impending attack; Hawkeye and Trapper sinking into a sex-starved funk. The girls on the couch laugh with the laugh track. Ellen thinks she could sew a pantsuit inspired by Major Houlihan's uniform—though she wouldn't be allowed to wear it to class.

Finally, the phone is hers. She slips into the semi-private alcove and sits on a wobbly three-legged stool. Guiltlessly, she reverses the charges to her parents. When a congested young man answers the phone at the base, Ellen asks for Sam and waits, immune to the voices in the background, the performance of rowdy lechery.

Sam calls her *baby* and she slides from the stool to the floor. "I talked to the bishop today," he says.

"And?"

"He thinks I can get baptized soon."

She is desperate for Sam to convert. Her desperation extends beyond her desire for him—although that desire, by itself, is insurmountable. During morning devotionals she lets her mind return her bare feet to the cold sand, Sam's hand to her ribcage. Otherwise, the amplified drone of the brother or elder or assistant to the quorum will bring Ellen back to her childhood. She will remember her older brothers brandishing a fire poker; the impact of steel against her teeth. When she was younger, they pinned her to the ground and forced their hands up her skirt. "Tell anyone and we'll kill your dog," they promised. She loved her dog and she believed them.

Still, she told her mother, "There's something wrong with James and Earl. The way they treat me isn't normal."

LaVerne, popular at church, was aloof at home. She had a curly helmet of hair and glasses that took up half her face. After birthing seven children in fifteen years, she looked older than she was. In lieu of booze or tobacco, she nursed an addiction to Tab.

"Please stop whining," she told her daughter.

If a boy like Sam is willing to convert to Mormonism, then the church can't be that bad. And if the church isn't that bad, then neither is LaVerne's coldness, her deference to her half-grown sons. Once married, Ellen will stop resisting religion. The best person she knows will be there with her saying, *yes, we believe this.*

Marriage will mean a clean getaway. Rexburg, Idaho is not a place where she can be happy. Mormons may pride themselves on having crossed mountains and conquered deserts—on settling where no man was meant to thrive—but not Ellen. The realization that she hates Ricks College descended as quickly as snow on the Tetons, which guard the flat, charmless campus. Her grades are bad. She is cold all the time. She is never alone.

And while she adores two of her roommates—stylish Lisa from Berkley, who loves disco and drives a Datsun; Tamar from Fiji, who exudes warmth and bubbles over with stories—six girls in one apartment induces a familiar restlessness. Ellen is, by nature, reclusive. She misses her red trailer and McLoughlin Boulevard. She misses her car, her freedom.

Her Human Development professor began the semester by quoting a poem: "The hand that rocks the cradle rules the world."

Ellen has no evidence that LaVerne rules the world—nor any evidence that LaVerne ever bothered to rock a cradle. Girls in class nodded their heads, took notes. Ellen is seventeen: though she's trusting marriage to save her, she harbors only the vaguest vision of herself as someone's wife, let alone someone's mother.

When Sam invites her to Tucson for Christmas, she accepts without hesitation.

*

I dropped out of high school when I was sixteen. No one ever believes it was your idea, but I remember. It was late and we were in the hot tub that strained the deck of the house on Long Street. The straps of your swimsuit were royal blue. Your hair stayed dry in a rare ponytail. From the deck we could see across the river to the Oregon City bluff. I told you I hated school, that being there made me want to crawl out of my skin. I wished there was a way to quit.

You said, "There probably is a way."

Unlike you at the same age, I did not petition the school board to give me a diploma. Graduating early was something I half-heartedly discussed with a guidance counselor; when he said it wasn't possible, I left anyway. I took the GED test at Clackamas Community College. For a few months I lived at home and drove Pat's old Jetta to work at the Subway on Macadam Avenue. Later I got a job as an administrative assistant in an architecture firm downtown.

It was 2006. Andy and Pat had already left home. Dad and I weren't getting along. Primarily because we shared a personality: we were both hazardously moody; we both insisted on controlling the emotional temperature of whatever room we were in. The two of you were still Republicans, still Christians. That I was increasingly wary of religion gave Dad so much palpable anxiety, I avoided him.

I moved out. You and Dad co-signed the lease on my studio and helped me borrow thousands of dollars from the government. I enrolled at Portland State University.

For years, the reason I dropped out of high school would change each time someone asked. The reasons ranged from academic to scandalous, mundane to cinematic. Now that I'm twice as old as I was then, the truth seems to be that I was a child desperate to grow up. I had tried all the things designed to distract a teenage girl from the condition of being a teenage girl—projects I hid from you, secrets I will keep from Wes. None of it made the daily tedium or soul-crushing social dynamics of high school bearable. My objective was to fast-forward adolescence and arrive at adulthood. I wanted to live alone, or with a boyfriend. I wanted a book deal, a German Shepherd, to sit on a fire escape and drink an entire bottle of wine.

Maybe leaving school was nothing more than a kid's impulsive experiment. What happens if I exit the building and never come back? What happens if I break the promises implicit in my ordinary middle-class childhood?

The question that interests me now is why you let me.

1975

Ellen flies to Tucson. She stays with a family Sam met through his new church. Sam gives her a tour of Davis-Monthan, all gravel and palm trees, rows of silver airplanes basking in the sun. For the first time in months, Ellen's cheeks turn pink. Her sadness, which in Rexburg cloaked and clung to her, evaporates.

She's in love with Arizona. At least, she's in love with the boy who brought her here.

On her last night they drive into the high desert, toward the Catalinas. Wrapped in a blanket on the hood of his car, they watch the sun slip down and the sky catch fire. Sam produces a ring set with three small diamonds. He tells her he's been baptized. His father is furious and his mother can't stop crying. But he loves her. He's certain. And so, for her, he has joined The Church of Jesus Christ of Latter-day Saints.

They will get married. They will have a family and live forever.

Our first interview begins with nervous laughter: yours, then mine. The video recording switches between our faces depending on who's talking. Initially my bedroom is bright and in focus, but I'm sitting in the dark by the time you say, "He had a diamond ring and the whole thing."

Behind me, my dog Hank noses open the bedroom door and approaches the webcam, white-tipped tail wagging. Dan appears and you wave him over. You ask about his first week teaching at Yale—was it weird, meeting with his students online?

"It was a lot like this," he says.

As soon as Dan leaves, you return our conversation to the Arizona desert. "So, yeah, that was the first marriage proposal I ever accepted."

I say, "*Oh,*" and write something down.

"But it didn't last very long. A few months later he broke it off with me and married someone else."

"Did you give the ring back?"

"I think I did. It was, like, a four-hundred-dollar ring. It was really pretty."

"Do you remember him breaking up with you?" I ask.

You say you remember it vividly, but when I press you for details—what you were doing when the phone rang, the words Sam used to cushion the blow—you come up with nothing. I understand it's the emotion that remains vivid. A boy dumped me when I was fifteen, and I'm not sure if he did it over the phone or online or in his car. All I remember is crying into a bath towel and that it was the spring I wore a pair of brown leather clogs to school every day.

You say, "I did somehow get a hold of a picture of the girl he married. I don't know if he sent a picture or—"

I'm shocked by this. "How would you have gotten a picture without, like, Instagram?"

"I don't know," you say, shaking your head and reaching for your wine. "I still have it somewhere."

1976

While Ellen commits to memory the smug, radiant face of the non-Mormon girl Sam has married instead of her, the freshly-built Teton Dam, eighteen miles from Ricks College, fills with water. In the spring, snow melts from the mountains. Now the dam fills at a rate its engineers did not anticipate. On the morning of June 5, 1976, the dam springs a leak. By noon the entire structure has collapsed.

Grainy water the color of instant coffee floods the Teton River, the Snake River Plain. On its way to Rexburg the deluge collides with a lumberyard, propelling logs toward town where they crack open a tank of gasoline and set floodwaters ablaze. Ricks College, built on higher ground, is quickly converted into emergency housing for those who evacuated in time. The rest of Rexburg is under water, on fire. Knocked from their foundations, houses set sail. Animals drown and their corpses tangle with the limbs of uprooted trees.

Ellen is already gone.

In her second semester, heart in pieces, she applied to nursing school at BYU. It was her second time applying but her first time getting in. She left Rexburg, Idaho the morning of June 1st, convinced she would never go back.

*

You left home in 1974 and gave birth to Andy in 1983. I left home in 2006 and gave birth to Wes in 2017. Do you know the years in between were the happiest of my life? There were book deals, and bottles of wine, office jobs to which I remained happily indifferent, a boyfriend I worshipped, then married, and an eighty-pound dog who is at least part German Shepherd (and sighing beneath the table as I write this). The life about which I'd fantasized at sixteen was mine, and I still think I could have lived within its boundaries forever.

I never recognized that life as a gift you had given me. In fact, those were the years when I believed I needed you least. When I thought nothing of going six months without seeing you and told you, over the phone, I was too busy to come home for Christmas.

It's October in Connecticut. As I write this, Dan is shut inside the bedroom teaching a class over Zoom. Wes is at preschool, our first taste of childcare in all his three and a half years. His teachers are concerned. He doesn't talk much. He struggles to answer open-ended questions—"Who lives with you at home?" "What do you do on the weekend?"—and is incurably restless during circle time. Last week, his teachers urged me to have him evaluated. I submitted the paperwork to the Yale Child Study Center, then went for a run, crying through the last two miles.

The leaves here are changing, and the tree-lined streets of

New Haven evoke the promises of a glossy college pamphlet. I don't want to be here.

It's useless to tell you this now, but I regret every time I didn't come home.

<<<<>>>

1976

She spends the summer in Ontario, a rural town at the Oregon-Idaho border, to which her parents moved a year ago. She works two jobs. For the Bureau of Land Management, she answers phones, files reports, and tracks the status of smoke-jumpers: firefighters who leap from helicopters and parachute through columns of smoke. They turn up at the Vale District Office in their bright jumpsuits, ash-stained helmets tucked beneath their arms. One by one, the men give Ellen their names and she marks them as safe.

From the office she drives straight to her babysitting gig. She's not wild about small children. The chaotic routine of their needs and demands is deeply familiar to her, and when she's with them, some essential edge of herself is effaced. Still, it's easy money, and the kids are sweet.

One day in July the dad comes home early. Digging through his wallet for cash, he gestures for Ellen to move closer to him. Abruptly he lurches forward and attaches his lips to hers. Her shame is profound; she hasn't yet recovered from waiting in line at the post office to mail her engagement ring back to Sam. To be kissed by someone else's husband is the last thing she wants. She quits.

In her car, the radio cuts in and out. Inevitably the song emerging from the static is "Don't Go Breaking My Heart." To distract herself, she sings along with Elton John and Kiki Dee.

In the early sun-baked evening, her parents' house is silent. Squalid. The house outside of Portland, in which Ellen grew up, was cluttered and unswept, but here LaVerne maintains no boundary between home and farm. Manure streaks the linoleum. Coarse hairs cling to the sink. Ellen ought to scrub the layer of grease from the stovetop, or throw out the spoiled milk—unpasteurized, straight from the cow—before someone gets sick. Instead, she drains a glass of tap water and watches flies buzz around a bowl of brown bananas. Cigarette smoke, her father's constant sacrilege, hangs in the air.

LaVerne works at the frame shop in town, and the family survives on her small paychecks plus Earl Sr.'s social security and pension (of which the church takes ten percent). Lucas and Tommy, ages thirteen and sixteen, are out hunting, or fishing, or tearing machinery apart with their hands. And the twins—Ellen doesn't know where the twins are. Supine in the grass somewhere, their hair unwashed, five-year-old faces aflame with chronic staph infections.

With a pang of guilt, or grief, she remembers her mother's pregnant belly. LaVerne's doctor never noticed she was carrying twins, and so it was with confusion that Ellen pressed on her mother's abdomen and felt, through thick uterine walls, a few too many limbs. An arm, a leg, an arm. Another arm. A few more legs.

She doted on the twins when they were born. At age fourteen she changed their swollen diapers, made their bottles, burped them on her bony shoulder. She rushed home from school to lift them from their shared crib and stare into their otherworldly eyes. She was especially proud of Elizabeth, her only sister. But she hasn't lived with the twins since they were toddlers, and now they barely know her.

This summer is not what she wanted. Her family regards her with a mix of indifference and suspicion. A boy was prepared to marry her, and now he won't? There is no question, in their minds, she did something wrong.

*

Our interviews last two hours and take me an entire day to transcribe. I save the recordings to my hard drive, email them to myself, and back them up to the cloud. I want to keep these files for the rest of my life. Sometimes I take a screenshot of the two of us. Moments when we touch our hair at the same time or laugh much longer than a joke deserves.

What you want to tell me is not always what I want to hear. I want to know how tall Sam was, and what his voice sounded like. Whether you installed a cassette player in your Toyota Corolla before you drove to Utah and what your parents argued about in their grubby kitchen. These facts seem critical to my ability to tell your story. I've written four novels; I can write a girl falling in love with a boy. I just need to know what kind of shoes he wore.

But I can't force you to fill out an autobiographical Mad Lib. Together we pull at the threads of your memories. The same events unravel slightly differently, depending on the night.

Halfway through our first interview, you again mention the speakers Sam gave you before he left for Tucson. "I held onto those forever," you say.

I doubt this. You couldn't have driven a massive seventies sound system from Portland to Rexburg to Ontario to Provo and, years later, back to Portland. But you say you did. I ask where the speakers are now.

"In Pat's living room," you say. "They sound great."

To supplement your selective memories, I spend an afternoon reading the 1975 course offerings from Ricks College—now BYU-Idaho—preserved in BYU's digital archive. I watch footage of the Teton Dam collapsing. I look up Billboard charts from the summer of 1976 and, on a long run, listen to "Don't Go Breaking My Heart" three times.

I tell myself these details are important, as they would be to a novel. At the same time I worry I'm making the book feel gauche and contrived, like a Civil War reenactment, but of your life.

If the Teton Dam mattered, wouldn't you have brought it up yourself?

*

I ask if you think LaVerne was depressed.

"I'm sure," you say. "The earliest memory I have of my mom is her pushing me away when I was distraught. I never felt like she loved me. Not in that kind of motherly, nurturing way."

I ramble about the fact that your mother had seven children. I use the phrases "psychological toll" and "lack of resources." Watching the recording the next day, my little lecture embarrasses me. It's so clear I'm trying to say something—or avoid saying something—about myself. Which is that, in your description of LaVerne, I recognize my own coldness. The glazed, faraway look in my eye that Wes must dread. The tensing of my body when he races across the apartment just to crash into my knees and laugh.

"Do you think your mom was depressed?" I ask, looking up at the ceiling as if doing math in my head.

Was I depressed in our small house in Ohio, when my six-month-old wouldn't nap and I buried my teeth in my own arm? A few days later, my publisher asked for an author photo and I had Dan take one of me leaning against the wooden fence in our sprawling backyard, the bruise on my biceps a purple moon I didn't bother hiding. Was I depressed when I threw a penguin-shaped sippy cup across our apartment in Richmond after begging my two-year-old to use words, any word, any sound that wasn't a prehistoric shriek?

I can count on one hand my memories of you raising your voice at me, or appearing even momentarily to resent my presence. Your love for me was palpable, like sun-warmed sand or a shaggy dog. I knew it was unconditional; you didn't have to tell me.

The more we talk about your childhood, the more I find myself saying to Wes what ought to go without saying. *I love you; I'm sorry; I messed up.*

I'm sorry; I messed up; I love you.

I don't want there to be any confusion.

1976

In Provo they stay up late watching *Saturday Night Live*. Ellen and her new roommates laugh at Chevy Chase's pratfalls, at Laraine Newman reporting live from the dicey Blaine Hotel. During a skit mocking the 1976 presidential debate, Lily Thompson as moderator prompts Chevy Chase as President Ford: "Rebuttal?"

"No, thank you," he demurs. "I just had dinner."

Some of the girls laugh conspicuously hard at punchlines about abortion, or Governor Carter's son smoking dope. Others sink into uncomfortable silence.

In the morning Ellen and her roommates and twenty thousand of their peers will join congregations all over town. On Tuesday they will sit through their weekly devotional. Last week, the twelfth president of the Mormon church, born in 1895, warned them about "the many hazards of interfaith marriage" leading to "the ugly dragon of divorce."

"Honorable, happy, and successful marriage," President Kimball warbled over the sobs of an infant in the back row, "is surely the principal goal of every *normal* person."

A month ago, a BYU graduate student submitted his dissertation on the effectiveness of electric shocks to the penis as a cure for homosexuality. Upon enrollment, Ellen and her roommates agreed to an honor code prohibiting coffee, tea, and tight clothing. They consider these rules, these beliefs, to be apolitical: it's God who hates the gays and condemns caffeine.

Still, in November, they will all vote Republican.

And still, unsupervised in the dorm lounge, irreverent sketch comedy makes them laugh until they cry.

James Taylor is tonight's musical guest. Ellen likes his angular face, his trim mustache, his overgrown sandy hair. The way he sings, *if it feels nice, don't think twice* as the camera pans to show him barefoot on stage. For the first time since she was fourteen, Ellen has no boyfriend. Her thumb is always folding over her palm, searching for the underside of an engagement ring.

Some weekends she drives from Provo to Ogden, where her brother Earl is stationed at the Hill Air Force Base. She drives an eleven-year-old Toyota Corolla her dad fixed up for her over the summer. Periodically the car overheats and she has to stop on I-15 to add water to the radiator. She avoids pulling over too close to the Utah State Prison, preferring maximum distance between herself and the incarcerated Ted Bundy. The way the Traverse Mountains loom above the sprawling complex gives her the creeps.

In Salt Lake she stops for clove cigarettes, which she'll smoke at her brother's house, never on campus. She shouldn't smoke at all—but isn't it a victimless sin? The crackle of the cloves, the numbing of her lips. If God can't forgive this small transgression, she's doomed.

At her brother's house she parks in the grass. Earl ambles from the open garage and listens to her describe her radiator's constant thirst. She envies the ease with which her brother manipulates the mechanical mess beneath the hood. Their dad taught the boys how to fish, hunt, and waterski. How to nurse an ailing engine back to health. Ellen never learned.

Inside, Earl's wife Candace, age twenty, is pulling a glass dish of cornbread from the oven. The girls are barefoot on the linoleum, fighting over a Sit 'n Spin. Toward her nieces—their manes of dirty-blonde hair, polyester nightshirts hanging to their knees—Ellen feels an overwhelming familial warmth. She hopes to know them all their lives. Candace punctures the crust of the cornbread with a toothpick. Satisfied, she leans against the counter and cracks her second beer. Soon Earl will come in from the garage and catch up fast.

Earl's time in the Air Force has eroded the edges of his faith. Ellen doesn't know precisely what her brother still believes, or how many rules he's willing to break. And she won't ask, unprepared to answer those questions herself.

While Candace is putting the girls to bed, Earl lights up a joint, which he doesn't offer to share. Ellen doesn't mind. Fast approaching is the hour at which he and Candace will either melt into each other at one end of the corduroy couch or begin fighting. Theirs are fights that ricochet from room to room before spilling into the backyard and merging with the weather. When Earl raises his voice, he reminds Ellen of their dad searching for his belt.

Tonight, she has brought along an offering. A distraction. Some of her more adventurous friends at BYU are getting into jazz, and Ellen loves nothing more than tearing the plastic from a new record. Candace reappears just as she's dropped the needle on Chuck Mangione's *Chase The Clouds Away*. Her brother and sister-in-law, Lynyrd Skynyrd fans, exchange weirded-out glances halfway through the title track—but they humor her, letting the album play to its end.

"Okay," Earl says. "Not bad. What else did you bring us?'

Maybe she doesn't need affection from her mother or attention from her father. Maybe it's not her fault her parents produced more children than they could convincingly love. This might be enough.

*

Brigham Young University—owned by The Church of Jesus Christ of Latter-day Saints—maintains a vast digital archive. The fastidiousness with which they have documented every dance, concert, lecture, forum, and assembly held on campus in the past hundred years hints at a motive beyond organization. I'm reminded of LaVerne's genealogy hobby, her obsession with determining her lineage (and with identifying any godless ancestors the church might baptize by proxy). Do Mormons believe that by keeping a record of life at BYU, they are writing history?

In a matter of seconds, I can access video, audio, and a transcript of the particular devotional you would have sat through on a given Tuesday in 1976. It's much harder to determine what you might have said to your brother, or he to you, through a haze of marijuana smoke three days later. I'm limited by your memories. By my understanding of who you were and later became.

A perk of writing nonfiction is the option of padding a narrative with research. To ground each scene in a verifiable time and place. But as a writer, I've always had to force myself to consider time and place. What naturally interests me is what people say to each other.

If this were a novel, that scene in Ogden would not end there. Instead, a nightmare would wake one of Earl's daughters; Candace would leap from the couch and exit the room. You would accept the joint from your brother's fingers and disarm yourself with a deep, mollifying drag. By the time Earl, drunk and high, began his apology, you would be half willing to hear it.

"For what we did to you," he would say. "We were stupid kids. And it was James's idea, you know, not mine. We had no clue how wrong it was."

"I forgive you," you might have said with experimental force. Because forgiveness was the gift of your religion—receiving it, bestowing it. "Life in that house wasn't easy for any of us. You didn't know what you were doing." And wasn't that the truth? No one had talked to you about sex, and no one had ever tried to convince Earl and James that their sister was their equal. If anything, your parents, and certainly the church, made a case for your inferiority.

Earl said, "You're always welcome here, you know."

"Thanks," you said, reaching again for the joint as Candace returned. The offer of a place to stay, an open door, meant more to you than Earl's watery apology. What you most wanted was the sensation of coming home, the ability to associate being loved with a street address. And for a period of time in 1976, your brother provided that.

Except he didn't. He offered you no lifelines; I made that up. In your memory, he never apologized. In your memory, you and Earl never talked much at all. So what do you mean when you tell me the two of you had a "connection?" Why am I trying to write that connection into existence?

I don't have five brothers, but I have two. In 1993 Andy accidentally elbowed me in the face and refused to get on the school bus until my nose stopped gushing blood. In 2005, while you and Dad were out of town, I didn't come home until four in the morning; as I stumbled toward bed, Pat emerged from his room to make sure I was okay. When Andy's first marriage ended, July 2008, the three of us plus Dan drove to the high school in Canby to watch fireworks. We lay in the grass smoking cigarettes and cracking sad jokes about our brother the twenty-four-year-old divorcé. The Mazda broke down in June 2020, two nights before we needed to move from Virginia to Connecticut. I called Pat and he wired me the money for a down payment on a new car.

Do we have a connection? We don't talk that much. I would kill for them.

Would any of your five brothers have killed for you?

*

I am writing a book about your life, and I don't know how close I should stick to the facts. I don't know what to illuminate or to hide. It's tempting to write in scenes that didn't happen—to give you what you never got. A related compulsion is to demand we revisit the same time periods again and again until I understand every glossed-over claim, all the inexplicable events that cling to your memory but raise more questions than they answer.

Sometimes when we're talking, you remember I haven't

asked these questions out of sheer curiosity. You preface your next story with, "You can't put this in your book—" before telling me something I desperately want to put in my book.

Do I believe that by recording your life, I am writing history?

Over Zoom, I tell you what I remember about Earl's death.

We were at Papa's house, which was now Papa and Nana's house (a few years earlier your in-laws, long-divorced, had married each other for the second time). I was in the back room watching television or talking to friends on the internet. I was fourteen. Everyone in the living room fell silent, or maybe you gasped. Something compelled me to rejoin the group. When I found you, you were flat on the floor crying into the phone.

At this point in the recording, you squeeze your eyes shut behind your glasses. My hair, cut pandemic-style with the kitchen scissors, falls into my face.

"Your grief didn't really add up, in my mind," I tell you. "Because I barely knew who this person was. I couldn't have picked Earl out of a lineup. And I don't think you ever really asked us to think of your family as the same as our family."

"No," you say, with neither pride or regret. "I didn't."

*

On November 2, 2003, your brother died in Iraq. He had left the Air Force several years earlier and was working as a private contractor, defusing bombs and disposing of munitions for the U.S. Army Corps of Engineers. He had taken the job for the ample paycheck—which would have allowed him to retire to the Philippines with his second wife. But the work was more danger-ous than advertised. A few weeks in, he wrote to his siblings that he doubted he would make it out alive. Three weeks later, Earl's convoy was diverted while he and his colleagues were trying to return to a base camp outside Baghdad. A bomb detonated be-neath the vehicle carrying your brother. His death was instant.

You were not close with your siblings. But in the days before Earl was killed, you were in constant communication with them. In his emails, Earl insisted there was nothing he could do to get out of his contract. Still, James was on the phone with state senators and officials from the U.S. Embassy in Iraq, fran-tically trying to bring your brother home. You tell me you had a bone-deep suspicion Earl would die. You compare your dread to the feeling we all had at the start of the pandemic: "when you know you're in such big danger, but no one can seem to stop it. So you just watch it happen."

Your grief is beginning to add up in my mind. When you say you and Earl had a connection, you mean you found a way to love him. You loved his daughters, and his attention to your car. You loved him for answering the phone and saying, "Come over." (Were you not supposed to love the people who had abused you? Were you supposed to love no one?) When your sister called with the news that Earl was dead, you were as shocked as if there had been no buildup, no warning. You fell to the floor; you sobbed into the phone.

In the last few years, you had undergone treatment for thy-roid cancer. Dad had closed his music store; you had been forced to sell your house. Did Earl's death cause your rocky young adulthood to fuse with the emergencies of middle age, as if nothing good had happened in between?

At fourteen, I had a forehead spangled with acne, long hair

I'd destroyed with a flatiron, and nameless ambition I steered toward restrictive eating. There was rarely a boyfriend but always a boy. He would be three or four years older than me, with a drug habit or a blog, a car, an actual girlfriend whom he would take to the prom. It wasn't that I longed for a less distracted mother. I didn't want you scrutinizing my lies, verifying I was "doing homework at the library" as often as I claimed. But I also didn't want you crying on the floor.

Do you remember my meltdown after he died? I claimed I had no clothes to wear to school, that I hadn't been shopping since the start of eighth grade, a year ago. Most likely you were not denying me new clothes, but trying to delay a trip to the mall by a month or a week. Maybe just a day. I cried, invoking my own ugliness. I used the line that had always worked on you: "We never spend any *time* together."

You took me to G.I. Joe's, a Pacific Northwest retailer that was later sold to Dick's Sporting Goods. I picked out some jeans, some gray T-shirts, and an oversized United States Air Force sweatshirt. I'd like to say the sweatshirt was a tribute to your dead brother, who spent more than half his life in the Air Force, but I doubt it. As a fashion choice, the sweatshirt would not have been out of place at my American high school in a politically moderate suburb soon after the 2003 invasion of Iraq.

Not a tribute, but tone-deafness. Was I oblivious to your grief?

At Earl's funeral, his daughter pressed play on a boom box. "Free Bird" filled the church—all nine minutes of it. You wouldn't look at me.

*

Lately you have been talking about retiring. You're a Nurse Manager at Oregon Health & Science University, where you've worked since you were twenty-two. Now you're in your sixties, still employed full-time during a pandemic. In September, you arrive at work to find the hallway crowded with premature infants asleep in their incubators. Due to wildfires, preemies were evacuated from hospitals in southern Oregon—but there's no room for them in the NICU. The sight of them in the hall makes you feel faint. You've been having trouble sleeping. Sometimes I text you at 6 a.m. on the East Coast, and you respond.

One day in October, you tell me you have filled out your retirement paperwork. You know your boss will offer you incentives to stay, but you don't care. You're done. Forty years is enough.

As a child, it seemed my primary occupation was waiting for you. I would be at preschool or your sister's house or home waiting for the rumble of the garage door, like a puppy with my ears pricked, head tilted. And finally you would appear, wearing a fleece pulled over blue hospital scrubs, smiling at me. You're the only person in the world who has smiled every time I've crossed your line of sight.

When you tell me you're going to retire, it doesn't matter that I'm three thousand miles away, an adult with my own apartment to which you have no key. You've unlocked the door. You're home.

A week later, when you tell me you've changed your mind— you and Dad don't have enough money in savings; you need to wait until you're sixty-five and qualify for Medicaid—you have left again.

1977

The woman behind the front desk looks her up and down, calculating the sum of Ellen's long hair, flannel shirt, loose jeans, nervous expression, hiking boots. "Just you?"

"Just me," Ellen confirms, shifting her canvas backpack to one shoulder. "I'm a college student. I'm working for the BLM for the summer."

The woman's beauty parlor hair and oversized glasses remind Ellen of LaVerne. "Oh yeah? What's your job over there?"

"I'm not exactly sure." Ellen's laughter is forced.

"Hope they got you doing something safe." The woman cracks her gum and slides a key across the counter. "You're in cabin seven, honey."

Ellen drives across a gravel lot and re-parks outside one of a dozen small cabins. No one prepared her for the daunting emptiness of the country surrounding Burns, Oregon. Harney County is over ten thousand square miles, home to fewer than eight thousand people. The town itself is a collection of motels, mobile home parks, saloons and small, steepled churches—the grid of which abruptly cedes to the high desert. Sage thrives, stubborn and stark in the red sand. Mountains cast shadows when they feel like it.

Tonight, she does her best to ignore the stiffness of the motel bedspread—to disregard the stains on the carpet, the singed curtains, that scene from *Psycho* and the flimsy lock on the plywood door. She fixates on Sam. If he had married her last spring, they'd have celebrated their one-year anniversary by now. She doesn't want to talk to him, exactly, but she wants to know if he remembers her. If he ever compares those memories to the reality of his wife in bed beside him—and if that's a contest Ellen has ever won.

Working for the Bureau of Land Management is different this year. On her first day, her manager introduces her to Darryl, an old codger of a pilot who spends his days crisscrossing the skies above cattle ranches, taking note of downed or damaged fences. For Darryl's latest assignment he needs an assistant. Someone to sit in the second seat of his Cessna while he flies low over the Steens, surveying Oregon's last living herd of wild mustangs. Ellen's job is to count the horses and mark their location on a map.

She's not scared of Darryl, whose old-man belly strains against the pearl buttons of his denim shirt. She's not scared of the tiny fixed-wing, its paint charmingly checkered white and red. Ellen is unconcerned until, halfway through their first flight together, Daryl pops the cap from a prescription pill bottle.

"What are those?" she asks into her headset.

"Nitroglycerin," he answers, patting his chest. "For my pains."

She knows what nitroglycerin is. It's the same medication prescribed to her dad, whose heart is always threatening to kill him.

Her stomach drops—but she's familiar with fear. Fear has been her lifelong friend. She fixes her attention on the ground: the ponderosa pines at the base of the mountain, the ridged rock-faces, the tear-drop lakes and stubborn patches of snow. She is nineteen. She has never been east of Colorado. Everywhere she goes is the most beautiful place in the world.

*

When you tell me about your job counting wild horses for the BLM, a rural twang creeps into your voice. "They sent me up there 'cause I was *dumb*," you say. "No one else would go up in that plane! The guy had angina, he had heart disease. He was having chest pain in the air."

I recognize the twang. When you've been drinking and talking about your past, your vowels swallow your words. You drop your g's. Your circumstantial cowboy accent used to embarrass me, particularly when you were talking to Dan, who was born on the Upper West Side and never lets a consonant melt on his tongue. I wanted you to hear how you sounded to him. I wanted you to talk like a woman who had never been to Burns.

Now, I picture you boarding the old man's Cessna, young and dumb and brave, and I love the way you talk. I want to cheer you on.

More than that, I want to go with you.

1977

Ellen moves out of the motel and in with a soil scientist. Suzanna is shyer than Ellen, tall and awkward and not as pretty. Ellen likes her roommate as automatically as she likes all passionate people—whether they're hooked on Deep Purple or disco or different kinds of dirt. They share a double-wide at the edge of town. In the evenings after work, they heat up cans of chili and gossip about the men in the office. Ellen tells Suzanna about Darryl popping pills in the sky and Suzanna's eyes go wide.

"What are you going to do if he has a heart attack up there?"

Ellen sits at their half-circle table, knees pulled to her chest.

"Land the plane, I guess." She's been watching carefully. She's pretty sure she could do it.

Suzanna is dating a fellow scientist. He picks her up on Friday nights and takes her to the Palace Restaurant and Lounge, where the walls are covered in two shades of red carpet, cocktails are cheap, and the dance floor crackles with sand. At BYU, Ellen went on a few dates with Danny, the star of the basketball team, but he bored her. All he cared about was basketball and God. She worries she'll never fall in love again. She might always be alone. And it's not that she minds being alone; it's that falling in love is her favorite activity. It's the thing she's best at.

She first sees him on the tarmac, climbing out of a two-seater. He catches her watching and lifts a hand as if they've known each other all their lives. His name is Casey Stratford. He is twenty-eight years old.

A Quality Control Officer at the local lumber mill, Casey flies for fun. With Casey she does all kinds of things for fun. They hike and drive and fly between mountain ranges, across national forests and over Indian reservations. They visit Vegas, the Grand Canyon, Death Valley, and eventually they fly to San Francisco to meet his parents.

Mr. and Mrs. Stratford are well-groomed, hydrated Californians who offer Ellen a glass of chardonnay and decline to ask how old she is. They ask instead about her family, and Ellen tells stories inspired by the truth: her dad long-retired and overseeing a modest farm; LaVerne a small-town socialite dabbling in genealogy and oil paints. Casey's parents (her future in-laws?) purse their lips and nod politely. Do they see through her lies? Not exactly. They see a teenage girl who never goes home.

Some weekends, the two of them stay on the ground, aimlessly burning gas in Casey's new Celica. From Burns they drive south through Hines and into the emptiness. They discover towns with populations in the single digits. Gas stations from which you can buy a homemade pie but can't make a phone call. In the mountains they hike to lakes—small and cold and thick with sediment. Relief from the heat. Ellen leans back, letting the water permeate her thick hair. Night falls and there is no order to the congregation of stars overhead.

She hasn't been to church in months. Once or twice she remembers this is all against the rules. Falling for another non-Mormon. Riding in his car and sleeping in his bed. Sitting on his kitchen counter, crossing one bare leg over the other while he teaches her to cook an omelet, to fold the egg without letting it break.

*

You take obvious pleasure in telling me about the Steens Mountain Wilderness. About wild horses and Casey's trailer. You're loose and amused, and so I decide to ask you something I've always wondered.

"Since you were still Mormon, were you abstinent?"

You say, "Um, no."

"Were you partially abstinent?"

You laugh at me. "What do you mean partially?"

I try again. "Were you having sex with Casey or not?"

"Yes. Totally."

"You're not a very good Mormon," I say, deflecting from my own embarrassment.

"I know that!" You're speaking for yourself now, but also then. You always knew. "I had this ideal I was trying to live up to. But no, I met Casey and it all went out the window pretty quick. We just had so much fun. He was amazing."

For every question I work up the nerve to ask you, there are ten more I can't manage, even as I know the book will be ridden with holes. As an author, I want these interviews to be rigorous, comprehensive, unflinching. But who flinches more than a daughter asking about her mother's sex life?

Was Casey your first? Was losing your virginity to him a choice—a difficult one to make? Were you guilty? Did you feel free? If it was only my own discomfort at stake, I might demand answers. But there is also your discomfort—and then there is our shared knowledge that this is not the hardest part of the story to tell. You and Casey careening around the desert is the good part. We are preserving our energy for what comes next.

1977

Something is wrong with Suzanna. Her pale hands shake as she opens a can of baked beans. Ellen kicks off her boots by the door. Sand scatters across the linoleum as she says, "What's the matter?"

Suzanna turns from the sink. "I'm pregnant."

Suzanna is a few years older than Ellen. She's mature, if not maternal. "Is that good news?"

Suzanna shakes her head. She needs an abortion. It's legal now, so long as you can get a doctor to say the pregnancy threatens your health—physical or mental. She can get it done in Eugene over a long weekend, then come back to Burns and fulfill the terms of her contract with the BLM.

"What about Mitch?" Ellen asks.

"We broke up. He doesn't want a baby. And I can't do this by myself. I know how it sounds, but I really can't."

When Ellen was thirteen, LaVerne, pregnant with the twins, went into labor months early. The same doctor who failed to detect multiple fetuses in her uterus—who prescribed amphetamines to stave off pregnancy weight—sent her home with two babies weighing seven pounds total. The babies sank deep into the folds of their hand-knit blankets, translucent eyelids closed tight against the world. Still, their amphibious fingers curled around Ellen's thumb. Still, their mouths popped open for milk.

Ellen is mad. At Mitch, and at the Supreme Court, and at the physician who will terminate her friend's pregnancy. "Aborting your baby won't fix anything," she tells Suzanna. "You're breaking your own heart."

Suzanna wasn't expecting Ellen's opposition, or her judgment. She has come to count on her roommate's warmth and curiosity and wide-open mind. Now, she's confronted with something else: Ellen's faith.

Ellen feels a surge of nausea, as if hers is the body brewing life. She sits at the table where she and Suzanna have often talked late into the night. The window reflects their anxiety back at them: the unwashed dishes stacked on the counter, Suzanna's hollow face and shoulders slumped in a sweat-stained, daisy-printed blouse. Selfishly, Ellen wishes her roommate hadn't told her. That Suzanna would do what she has made up her mind to do without implicating Ellen in any deadly sins.

As it is, Ellen feels compelled to stop her. "You'll regret it," she argues. Suzanna will be haunted by the ghost of her child: the phantom milestones and uncelebrated birthdays. And though Ellen hates to say it, hates to think it, the procedure will nullify Suzanna's chances of salvation. There's no abortion in heaven.

Ellen has always understood that Latter-day Saints are rare. Most people have rejected the Book of Mormon. In church, she was warned against bonding with these people. If they don't corrupt you with their disbelief, they go rigid when you explain the truth; they look at you askance, as if you're wrapped in newspaper ranting on a bench in downtown Portland.

The night Suzanna leaves for Eugene, Ellen packs up her things and moves into Casey's trailer across town. Lying across his unmade bed, she watches him brush his teeth in the bathroom. With lazy confidence he maneuvers the brush around each molar, savoring but not acknowledging her gaze. Casey is nearly a decade older than her. Not her husband, not even her fiancé. Ellen's own guilt is murky and difficult to parse. Does she regret their intimacy, inextricable from their love? Should she have tried harder to save Suzanna's baby?

She is old enough to draw a distinction between sins. Flavored tobacco is not as wrong as sex, and sex is not as wrong as murder. But at nineteen, she is not equipped to remake the world. She still craves the system passed down from her mother's mother to her mother, by which a girl can measure her own worth. She knows it's hypocritical, but she still believes in her potential to be good.

*

I've never had an abortion. When I was younger, I was terrified of needing one. In part because you raised me to believe in God and, as a teenager, when I first had the kind of sex that could result in pregnancy, I still kind of did. I took no comfort in the Holy Bible and had never leaned on the promise of life after death—heaven always sounded like hell to me—but I was afraid of its absence, the nullity of non-existence. I wanted to believe that if the plane went down, it mattered whether I prayed. Whether I generally deserved to live and not die.

The primary reason I was anxious about abortion was that you had impressed on me, intentionally or not, that ending a pregnancy was the worst thing a girl could do. Your pro-life conviction led you to vote Republican in every presidential election before 2012. When I was in high school, I asked you, "What if I was raped?"

"That would be horrible. It's the one situation that makes me think twice, but…" You looked into your wine glass. You shook your head.

Later that year, a close friend of mine got pregnant and decided to have the baby. You said you were glad she was taking responsibility for her actions. When I was eighteen, in love with the boy I would marry, I admitted to you I thought abortion should be legal. Available to anyone who wants one. You looked at me across the patio table and said, "Believe me, if you get pregnant, you're not aborting Dan's baby."

You may have been right.

Over time, as I grew comfortable with my own faithlessness, accepting a kind of existential chaos in exchange for freedom from the rules of Christianity—rules I resented for bleeding conveniently into Republican talking points—my fear was not of unwanted pregnancy, but of keeping one a secret from you. Telling you I'd had an abortion, I thought, would destroy our relationship. And so I would have to accept the cost of *not* telling you: no more wine-fueled conversations about the past. No more confessions on the tip of my tongue, waiting for our third or fourth glasses. Forever forced to keep my guard up.

The first time I got pregnant was on purpose, but I miscarried. The second time, the embryo stuck and Dan and I opted for the earliest and most accurate genetic testing available. If the results were devastating, I would schedule an abortion before the end of my first trimester. I considered waiting to tell you my news—but I couldn't. You were about to fly to Toronto to spend a week with me while Dan went backpacking in Wyoming. I knew I wouldn't be able to hide my nausea, or my joy. And on the off-chance I decided to end my pregnancy, I figured I could lie and say I'd miscarried again.

In Toronto, you and I rented a car. We drove north to a cabin in Restoule, Ontario. The road to the property was unpaved and uneven, disrupted by boulders embedded in the dirt. I pressed a hand protectively to my midsection as you drove. The Jeep rattled and lurched over the rocks. We made it to the cabin and I immediately got mad at you for forgetting to pack the bread. As I was puking canned chili into the long grass behind the outhouse, you received a call. Your sister's voice was spliced with static. LaVerne was dying in Texas.

You spent the afternoon on the screened-in porch, watching the rain hit the lake. Barely speaking, rarely moving, calmer and more contemplative than I've ever seen you, the calmest and most contemplative person I know

Before we'd left Toronto, I had promised you we would hear a loon. The bird is uncommon in the Pacific Northwest; you were unfamiliar with the sound it makes. I told you it would happen at sunset. But as the trees became silhouettes against the sky and no loons wailed, I second guessed myself. Maybe it was the wrong time of year for loons, or maybe I was wrong about where I'd heard one. Could have been western Massachusetts the year before, or even Minnesota in 2008, visiting Dan at college. I wanted to apologize, but you hadn't spoken in over an hour. It seemed safe to assume you'd forgotten.

Finally, before the last traces of daylight disappeared, we heard the saddest two notes echo across the lake. Hollow and haunting: the sound of one animal looking for another.

You turned to me, your eyes damp and bright: "Was that it?"

We were back in the city when my doctor called with the test results. "Low risk," she said. "And the fetus is male! Enjoy your visit with your mom."

It was only after we cried and I shook in your arms—a boy? A son?—that you told me Andy and Charlene were waiting on the same test. My sister-in-law was a month further along than me.

"If the results are concerning, they might have some tough choices to make." You looked me in the eye.

You said this swiftly, but deliberately, as if letting me off the hook.

*

You flew from Toronto to Dallas. Your sister Elizabeth, also a nurse, was already there. As you walked into your mother's hospital room, she smiled at you. You were washing LaVerne's hair when she died.

That night, you texted to tell me she was gone. I crawled into bed beside Dan and wept. Keep in mind I was always weeping. I was always taking pictures of my body in the mirror and believed, on some level, I was the first woman ever to be pregnant.

Also keep in mind: if I am stingy with grief, it's because I know my life will one day be undone by it.

Over Zoom, I ask, "Do you remember anything she said to you before she died?"

You laugh a little. "She kept saying, 'I wish the boys were here.'"

*

Lately, I haven't been sleeping. The 2020 election is four days away. Wes keeps throwing tantrums—because he doesn't want to wear a coat, or he wants to eat his crackers upside down on the couch, or the dog messed up his orderly line of Matchbox cars. I lie awake wishing I had handled myself better. That I hadn't yelled at him, or grabbed him hard by the shoulders and told him, "You're being bad right now. This is *bad*."

Last night I finally took two Advil PMs and sank into sleep. My dream took place in the one-bedroom house on 9th Street in Oregon City. You and I were upstairs in the attic, where you and Dad used to sleep, and you'd found a draft of this book. You marked it up with a red pen until ink overtook the text. You crumpled the pages and threw them at me. "You shouldn't have written it like this," you said. "This is not how it was."

I grabbed you hard by the shoulders and said, "I love you. You were a good mother. This is a story about you being a *good* mother."

Now, I stuff Wes into his coat while he rages, then I drop him off at preschool. The teacher who used to be his favorite greets him with forced cheer: Wes shies away. We're still waiting for the Child Study Center to review our paperwork—though part of me hopes they've mislaid the forms. At my core, I don't believe anything is wrong with my kid. (Won't he talk when he's ready? Sit still when he's older?) Or else I believe the cost of courting a diagnosis will be steeper than the cost of allowing him to be himself—primarily because Wes, at age three, believes he is perfect. How can he be wrong?

I go running in the cold rain, the fronts of my bare thighs stinging in a way that reminds me of my childhood, which was mossy, muddy, and damp. (Did you ever make me wear a coat?) Running south on Whitney Avenue, I take a left at Planned Parenthood, where protesters wave pictures of blood and tissue and take turns shouting into a megaphone. A young man in damp khakis holds onto the collar of a golden retriever who can't stop shaking water from her ears. The rest of these people are older, their clothing coded conservative. My options are to run straight through them, or stop and wait for traffic to clear so I can cross the street.

I keep running.

1977

They're engaged by the start of her junior year. Casey leaves his job at the lumber mill and starts grad school at the University of Chicago. When he visits Ellen in Provo, she waits until the other girls are studying in their rooms before sneaking Casey into hers. She's on birth control now. The pills ease her cramps and almost guarantee she'll never find herself in Suzanna's position. In the morning, they leave campus before anyone else is awake. Casey needs his two unholy cups of coffee.

Ellen skips church services and devotionals for cross-country skiing with Casey. Propelling herself across the snow, her arms and legs in fluid tandem, she's exhilarated to discover her own athleticism. Her endurance hints at another life, one spent at dizzying altitude, cold air filling her lungs. They drive though small towns, stopping in diners whose frozen parking lots are a surreal epilogue to their high desert summer. They reach across a Formica tabletop for each other's hands.

"Do you ever believe in God?" she asks him. Lately, faith either obsesses or eludes her. She wants God the way she wants sex: desperately or not at all.

A vague answer would satisfy her. As long as he believes in something on a day like this. If he feels humbled by the mountains or invincible when he looks at her—that none of this could possibly be an accident—she will consider their beliefs adjacent.

Knowing exactly what Ellen wants from him, Casey presses his knees against hers beneath the table. "No. And you won't always, either."

To him, her religion is a quirk, a childhood habit she'll soon outgrow. And she almost loves him enough to forgive the cruelty of that assumption. It's only when he leaves her alone in Provo that her doubts keep her up at night. That he's been seeing other women in Chicago doesn't help. Casually, he claims, seeming to regard their engagement as a plan for their future more than a condition of their current lives.

With his mouth full of pie, he says, "You're so much smarter than that."

To disappear into his life would be to shut the door on the only life she has inherited. If Ellen wants the temple wedding, her mother beaming, the adulthood she's been promised is right and righteous, she needs a different man. A boy her own age. Maybe a former high school quarterback fresh from his mission in El Salvador. Like the one who keeps looking at her across the aisle of the lecture hall where they both have American Literature. A boy like William Strout.

1978

It happens fast. Over the course of a single winter, William's assumptions become her lies. No, she doesn't have a secret fiancé in Chicago who pays her long-distance phone bills. Yes, she's a virgin. No, it doesn't bother her that the Book of Mormon diverges from the Holy Bible according to the whims of a polygamous self-proclaimed prophet. Yes, she's close with her brothers. No, she never convinced her high school boyfriend to renounce his church and join her own. Yes, she wants to get married and give birth to a half-dozen babies. No, she has never smoked a cigarette. Yes—and this part is true—she wants to drive with him to Twin Falls, Idaho and meet his family. To hold William's hand above the table and finish the prayer: *in the name of Jesus Christ, amen.*

*

When I was a kid, you talked to me about sex exactly twice. The first time I was eleven, lying on my stomach across the end of your king-sized bed watching *Touched by an Angel* with you and Dad. In "Cassie's Choice" (Season 1, Episode 5) a young Alyson Hannigan stars as a pregnant teenager. The actress's prosthetic baby bump is revealed a minute into the episode. Dad, sitting up in bed behind me, said, "That's what happens."

I craned my neck to look back at him.

"When you have sex," he finished.

I nodded to show I understood, was unbothered. I had looked up "sex" in the dictionary at the start of fifth grade. I was surprised the word seemed only to mean "either of the two main categories into which humans are divided on the basis of their reproductive functions." This was not the information I sought. My finger traveled down the page to "sexual intercourse." I read the definition once. Twice. I thought, *that can't be right.*

But a year had passed since then; the concept had marinated in my mind. I'd accepted the unseemly mechanics, and now I waited to see if Dad would say more. He did not. We watched in silence as Monica, the guileless white angel, disappointed Tess, the beleaguered black angel, by letting Alyson Hanigan escape the hospital with her newborn shortly after signing the adoption papers.

The second time either of you invoked intercourse, I was seventeen. I no longer lived with you. I told you I'd bought a ticket to New York to visit the boy I'd met at creative writing camp the year before.

Dad said, "As Christians, we think it's important to wait until you're married to have sex."

"I'm not planning to have sex in Dan's parents' house." I figured there were other places.

"I'm just saying. We both regret not waiting for marriage." He nodded at you, busying yourself in the kitchen. You cringed without looking at me.

I've claimed you talked to me about sex twice. But *you* did not: Dad did, while you more or less remained in the room. Later, when Dan and I and all our friends were adults gossiping over takeout containers while our babies slept upstairs, we compared notes on our own parents and how they'd raised us, ever-conscious of inching closer to the ages at which they'd frozen in our minds. I was the only one who could say my parents had never subjected me to "the talk." I'd known girls who were made to wear purity rings and girls who were directed to the Costco box of condoms in the linen closet, but none whose mothers had evaded the topic entirely.

At the time, I figured you'd underestimated me. You didn't think you were leaving me to navigate my sexuality on my own; instead, your silence suggested there was nothing to navigate. And you'd have been forgiven for assuming I had no interest in dating. My move was to have boys drop me off two blocks from home. I claimed to have been at the library, or at a friend's house, or on a long walk.

Now, I think back to you cringing in the kitchen. Maybe you knew Dad's warning was overdue and gratuitous. Maybe, by sparing me the talk, you meant to spare me the shame that had been forced on you since you were a child home alone with your brothers.

You didn't believe in my fundamental innocence. You believed I was fundamentally safe—and now I desperately want to end this section here; I don't want to prove that I was or was not safe. I don't want to become the main character of this story, even temporarily. What is the point of reminding you I was a teenage girl with long blonde hair and self-destructive impulses? What is the point of listing the times my rabbit-heart beat in my throat?

Compared to you, I was safe. Compared to yours, my childhood was a joy.

1978

Spring break approaches and Casey buys her a plane ticket to Chicago. William, who works as a rafting guide when he's not in school, invites her to tag along on a trip down the middle fork of the Salmon River. Instead of choosing between them, Ellen says yes to both.

When William asks why she's going to Chicago, she tells him about Suzanna. That her roommate from the summer has moved to Chicago is both a lie and a fantasy: Suzanna will never speak to Ellen again. Deceiving her boyfriend is easy. Having never met a girl with anything to hide, William's follow up questions are specific but totally unsuspecting.

As the plane descends over the city, Ellen feels sick. She paws through the seat-back pocket for a paper bag, but the sensation passes as the plane touches down. She's nervous to see Casey, afraid she'll be swept up in the ongoing adventure of his life—and equally afraid, this time, she won't be. Whether they're still engaged is unclear. Weeks ago, she interrogated him about Melanie, a girl he took cross-country skiing. Casey admitted the friendship is more than friendly, but insisted it doesn't change his feelings for Ellen. "When I'm with you, I'm with you," he told her. Easy as pie.

The ambiguity of their engagement lessens her guilt over seeing William behind Casey's back—or Casey behind William's. Guilt vanishes entirely when she sees Casey at the gate: tall and a little stooped, hands shoved into the pockets of his puffer vest, overgrown hair fringing his ears. She thinks, *my friend is here.*

Chicago isn't Burns, or Provo, or even Salt Lake City. Chicago is steel and wind chill, trains shuddering on their tracks. From the top of the Sears Tower, she sees the crease between the sky and Lake Michigan. "Look at the horizon." She savors the word.

"No mountains in the Midwest," Casey says. His hand is beneath her jacket, against the right side of her abdomen. His fingers press into the persistent and alien tenderness she's been trying to ignore. "You think you could live here?"

In this moment, she thinks she could live anywhere.

They go out for pizza. Casey orders a beer and asks why she doesn't want one. She tells him her stomach is upset, which is true. In fact, the pain is truer and more urgent than the necessity of not drinking because she may marry a Mormon boy.

William is so good. And while goodness bores her, William doesn't bore her. After two years in El Salvador, he speaks fluent Spanish. He studies more than anyone Ellen has ever met. For William, the highlight of the academic year is receiving his grades. He's convinced he's a good dancer, though he isn't. He's adamant he never needs a coat, though he does. His favorite color is brown.

Why is Ellen thinking about William as she sits across a table from Casey? Casey, who is either her best friend or big brother or the love of her life, is looking at her with concern. The pressure of the wooden chair against her spine is excruciating. Why does she wish it was William to whom she is admitting this? After faking it all day, she exposes her pain as unendurable.

"I need to go to the ER."

*

Ellen calls LaVerne.

"Can you come here?" she asks over the beeping of a heart monitor, through her fading morphine haze. Outside her window a construction crane swings so fast and erratically, she imagines the machine shattering the glass and knocking her out cold.

"Come *there*?" asks LaVerne, hanging onto a note of cheer.

"Chicago. I had my appendix out. Please? I want you to come."

She pictures her mother standing in the mustard-hued kitchen of their house in Portland. Ellen is unable to account for the passage of time, to conjure the mess of her parents' farmhouse in Ontario, which has never felt like home.

"What are you doing in Chicago?" LaVerne's tone is suddenly defensive. She spits the word *Chicago*.

"I was visiting a friend," Ellen says. Her friend wasn't in the room when she woke up from surgery. Casey appeared two hours later with a stuffed Snoopy from the hospital gift shop and the dejected air of a boy who didn't get what he wanted for Christmas. "I don't like hospitals," he tried to explain, pale at her bedside. "They make me claustrophobic."

"I'm on spring break," Ellen says, "and I started feeling really sick. So I went to the ER."

I want my mom, is what she means to convey. But her desire is increasingly divorced from the woman on the line. Is there someone else who goes by *Mom*?

A long pause. LaVerne could be locating her car keys, unlatching the pink rollers from her hair, instructing Tommy and Lucas to keep the twins alive.

"We'll pay the bill." LaVerne laughs a little. "Is that what you want me to say?"

*

I wasn't sure I wanted you in the room when I gave birth. The end of my pregnancy was, I sometimes think, the best time of my life. In hindsight it's embarrassing, the pride I took in my normal, healthy pregnancy. My body strong and lean, save for a contained bump; my sex life uninterrupted by the project of gestation; my five hundred square foot apartment with its corner of stacked diapers and folded onesies.

On Tuesday nights, Dan and I rode the Queen streetcar to St. Michael's Hospital in downtown Toronto. Our teacher was a piercingly funny doula who spent as much time warning us about postpartum depression as she did wielding a plastic pelvis, pointing out the dips and dives of the birth canal. On our way home, Dan and I would do impressions of our peers: the dad-to-be who raised his hand to ask—humorlessly, avoiding his wife's stare of disbelief—how fast PPD could spiral into psychosis. Or the couple who wondered aloud in thick Russian accents whether they ought to have used something other than olive oil for perineal massage. On the streetcar's red-upholstered seats, our boots grinding chemical salt into the floor, we laughed until I worried my convulsions would induce labor.

I was happy because I had Dan's undivided attention. Because nothing mattered to us except the baby, confirmation and extension of our love. Our son would make his entrance and delight us, as we'd been delighting each other since we were teenagers. I knew birth could be long and traumatizing, but I must have believed trauma was a trophy, a Girl Scout badge I was eager to earn. On some level I realized Dan would spend the first months of Wes's life finishing his dissertation and interviewing for academic jobs. What I didn't understand was how absolutely alone I would feel in the middle of the night, infant screaming in my arms as my husband slept in a New Jersey hotel room.

A baby confirms the love between two people—but not without coming between them. You must have known this. My due date approached and I wondered if I even needed you.

Twelve hours into labor, I called you. It was 3 a.m. on the West Coast. You answered the phone alert and excited.

"It's happening," I said.

You pulled up Air Canada's website. Your bag was already packed.

After landing at Pearson late in the evening, you took a cab to St. Michael's, where I had just been admitted. I had labored at home for twenty-four hours, at first eating bites of a chicken salad sandwich and taking frequent walks, crouching to greet neighborhood dogs, my contractions a secret. We called a cab when I could no longer catch my breath. The driver asked if I was okay and, after Dan explained I was in labor, passed me a bottle of water.

The hospital was cold and silent, like a shopping mall after hours. My confidence collapsed. I wanted drugs. You walked into the room as an inexperienced anesthesiologist was, for the second time, jamming an epidural into my spine. (Eventually, a senior physician would be paged for a third attempt, but he too, for reasons never explained to me, would fail.) You've told me that as you entered the room I started to sob. You weren't sure if I was crying from pain or relief.

I don't remember crying when you walked into the room. I remember a nurse saying either you or Dan had to leave; technically, the anesthesiologist was performing surgery, and his audience was officially too large.

I sent Dan away.

*

You never stopped wanting the mother you didn't have. Your brain was committed to the project of softening, forgiving, recasting LaVerne as someone who would come when you called (3 a.m., bag already packed).

Could she have redeemed herself in your eyes forever by getting on the next flight to Chicago? What if, at any point in your life, she had apologized? *I'm sorry; I messed up; I love you.*

"I'll never forget when I called her," you say. "Because she was never there! But somehow I still cried out to her."

"You thought she would come," I say.

"And you know, maybe she couldn't. But to me, at that time, it didn't matter if she *could* or not. She *didn't.*"

You say this to me over a late-night video call halfway through my fourth year of being Wes's mother. In the recording, my face registers your insight—the unavoidable, illogical trap of motherhood: it doesn't matter what we're capable of doing. It only matters what we do.

1978

Beneath her baggy sweater is a post-surgical hematoma. The blood will be reabsorbed in one to four weeks, her doctor promised. For now, her abdomen bulges like a pregnancy, the skin mottled black and yellow and blue. The pain requires ice and rest, her full attention—but Ellen does her best to ignore it.

Nothing will ever be the same with Casey, because his eyes went glassy when she needed him; his apartment, covered in maps and shrines to aviation, felt like the farthest place from home. She's sure if she hadn't gone to Chicago her appendix would not have burst, and she and William would be engaged by now.

She crosses the airport parking lot at dusk, searching for her Honda and repeatedly reaching inside her purse to touch her keys and water-warped checkbook. She finds her car just as a man, his limbs hanging from a pickup truck, shouts and waves at her.

"Miss? Hey, miss?"

She slams the car door and pushes down the lock. She follows signs for I-15 North. William expecting her tonight means she'll be there tonight. As she drives, her heart pounds in time with the nauseating pulse of the blood clot beneath her skin.

The sky is dark. Oncoming headlights make her head ache. What keeps her from falling asleep at the wheel is a premonition of vomit—a sensation worsened by the seatbelt digging into her bruise. At the last second, she veers west toward Twin Falls, where she shows up on her cousin's doorstep well past the bedtimes of Lacey's small children. Beneath the porch light, Lacey looks stunned.

"Can I crash here tonight? I'm on my way to Salmon to meet my boyfriend. But I'm tired. I was traveling for spring break and I'm just—I'm too tired to keep driving."

On the television behind Lacey, a talk show host compulsively shouts one-liners. Blue light bathes the living room walls. Lacey will press her for details, won't she? With a mother's intuition, Lacey will yank up Ellen's sweater and expose the hematoma. Maybe she'll tuck Ellen into bed and insist she stay for days. Call LaVerne and demand she come and collect her daughter. On some level, Ellen is desperate for her cousin to do these things.

"I'll leave first thing in the morning," she promises.

Lacey squints at her mother's sister's child. One of seven. "You sure you're alright?"

"Yes," Ellen says.

"Try not to wake the kids if you use the shower. Thin walls, you know." She steps aside, admitting Ellen into the house.

On a hide-a-bed, between musty sheets, Ellen rehearses the story she will tell William tomorrow and for the rest of their lives: Chicago. Suzanna. The Sears Tower and the slate gray lake. Pizza, pain, appendectomy. Everything is fine now. The bruise looks worse than it is.

*

You start to tell me about the Salmon River. You claim it was the most beautiful place you had ever been—a claim you've already made about the Steens Mountain Wilderness and the Columbia River Gorge. And then you interrupt yourself.

"While we were there, a really weird thing happened. We had friends from college who were living in Salmon, and they had a two-year-old. Except a day or so earlier they had accidentally run over their two-year-old in the driveway and killed him. William and I went through that whole thing together. We really bonded over that whole situation. It was horrible. It was one of the more horrible experiences I've ever had."

I have resisted this detail of the dead two-year-old. I have tried, several times, to write this book without him. I have no idea what he means.

In a novel, a dead two-year-old is an instigating event. He's the entire story—not a hazy detail befalling nameless side characters. In real life, other people's tragedies loom in the periphery, a threat of what might happen and a promise that it won't: how can it, when it already happened to them?

You can't talk about this period of your life without mentioning the two-year-old. You bring him up every time.

After sleeping at your cousin's house, you resumed driving to Salmon, where you met up with William. You don't remember where you stayed while you prepared for the rafting trip. You know you spent some amount of time with William's friends from college, who had killed their son. You say it was horrible—traumatizing to be near them. And yet, when I press you for details, you produce nothing. Who was driving the car? How many days before your arrival did the boy die? Why would this couple, in their profound grief, ever have invited you over? What role did you and William play in "the whole situation?" What did you say to each other about the death of a kid whom you had never met?

Mom, what are you talking about?

It feels like a failure on my part—my inability to tease out a narrative from this memory. Then I think about other stories you've told me: the teenager in the ICU, crushed by a city bus, almost without legs, looking up at you and asking, "Will I be okay?" Or the boy wheeled into the ED with an archery arrow protruding from his eye socket. Or the toddler who took his final ventilated breath in the Covid unit last week.

At age twenty, you were still in nursing school. You were beginning to understand your life would always be adjacent to other people's tragedies. A nurse sometimes watches children die, then drives home and pretends (to her own children, if not to herself) that youth defies death. Maybe you already realized you would spend your life mourning people you'd never known.

Maybe it was important to you that your husband have the same capacity.

1978

She falls in love again. With the fitful Salmon River slicing through the Sawtooths. With William's arms flexing as he braces an oar against white rapids. Over the course of a week, alpine peaks melt into bare, brown hills, which steepen into a gorge lined with granite. She learns to expect the water crashing into the boat, shockingly cold, soaking her legs and the edges of her shirt. Her abdomen remains swollen, revoltingly tender. When she climbs into the raft—after the group has stopped to hike or soak in the hot springs carved into the riverbank—she ties the dirty yellow strings of her lifejacket and smiles up at William.

"This is amazing," she says.

He kisses her in front of everyone. The tourists, who have paid to be ferried down the Salmon River's middle fork, cheer for the couple, rehearsing for a proposal that feels imminent. What Ellen wants to ask William, but never does, is whether they can take this trip again someday. When she's not in so much pain.

In the evenings, the guides unload guitars and tarps and fishing rods from the belly of a raft. They set up camp, complete with pots for boiling water, a grill to place over the fire, knives for splaying fresh-caught fish. She showers beneath a waterfall or climbs alone to a ridge to see the sun drop into the canyon. Deer gather at dusk to drink from the river. To distract herself from her discomfort, she imagines calling LaVerne the moment she gets back to BYU.

"I'm engaged," she'll say.

"Oh yeah? Again?" LaVerne will withhold enthusiasm until Ellen confirms the boy's status: Mormon. Pre-med. Mission completed.

To get back to camp, she follows the sound of William holding court around the fire: ghost stories and Neil Young covers. Casey was serious, boyish. William is goofy and unguarded. Younger, yet more of a man.

On their last night, a fever sends her to bed early. Wrapped in all the clothes she brought with her, she lies in her sleeping bag and fails to sleep. She squeezes her eyes shut and focuses on the fantasy of calling her mom. Together they pick out a pattern for Ellen's wedding dress. They enter the fabric store and LaVerne grips her daughter's arm, murmuring, "Oh, I'm in heaven."

The fantasy feels flimsy, unsatisfying and unlikely. Ellen reaches for William's canvas backpack. The group sings "Highway in the Wind" as the temperature slips: *Love me while you have me, babe.* She rifles through her boyfriend's stuff, looking for secrets to rival her own. Cigarettes, or a picture of another girl. Anything he's never told her would be a relief. But all she finds is a Swiss Army knife, a compass, a diamond ring in a velvet box. She spins the compass between her fingers until it's too dark to see the dial.

When the light from William's lantern bobs through the trees, she's wide awake. He crouches beside her on their tarp, presses the back of his hand to her forehead.

"Fever?"

"Just badly sunburned." The Idaho sun had been pure and intense, reflected in the white rapids, searing her vision.

"You're clammy."

"Maybe a low-grade fever? They said that might happen."

He pushes her damp hair from her face. "I'll take care of you."

She believes him.

*

You became a nurse. Over your forty-year career you have worked in Adult Critical Care, Pre-Op, Interventional Radiology, and Vascular Access. You became a Nurse Manager for the Vascular Access, Apheresis, and Wound-Ostomy teams. Now you run the Inpatient Diabetes Education and Center for Women's Health.

You also became, as an adult, the person other people want taking care of them: your children. Your husband's parents. Friends with cancer diagnoses. Your pregnant daughters-in-law. Even Dan, sick with Rocky Mountain Spotted Fever in the summer of 2019, wanted you. The obvious explanation is you're a professional. You caretake for a living. But isn't it the other way around?

Didn't you become a nurse because you were already calm, confident, self-effacing, and comfortable with bone-deep fear? Caretaking for you was intuitive. It was synonymous with survival.

You had spent your whole life taking care of yourself.

<<<>>>

I married Dan three days after my twenty-first birthday. (I wanted to be able to drink at the wedding.) I had never believed in God less than in those days. I would have told you I believed in the perfection of Dan's wrist bone, and in the Columbia River snaking through the gorge. The way a dog's head wrinkles as she bends forward. To finally believe in nothing else was a relief, a joy. Shaking off that weight was not unlike falling in love.

You didn't teach me this. You taught me to pray. To ask God for forgiveness. To let Jesus into my heart—a process that seemed formal yet came with no instructions, resulting in me crouching behind the couch in slants of afternoon light, requesting forgiveness again and again, worrying that each time negated the last.

You let me amass a menagerie of pets: rodents, rabbits, cats, a puppy. Pat still remembers, with amused disgust, the shelves of books and rows of birdcages lining my childhood bedroom. You let me check out twenty paperbacks from the library and left me alone to read them in the backyard, a bag of potato chips for dinner. You never made me wear a coat. You loved my friends and loathed my enemies and accepted, without question, when one became the other. You let me drop out of high school. Gradually, and while suppressing your devastation, you stopped making me go to church.

Did you pave the way for my faithlessness?

Does a girl, permitted to do as she pleases, have any use for God?

*

I was not the first of your children to get married young. At age nineteen, in a yellow thrift store dress, in the kitchen of your house on Troon Drive I announced I was getting married and Andy, already divorced at twenty-five, choked on his beer. Weren't you wary of engagements by then? Did you not want to yank the ring from my finger?

About the ring: it was set with a single violet pearl Dan and I had found in a mussel we pried from a rock in Maine (and which Dan, drunk, nearly swallowed). We were on spring break with our friend Cooper in a house borrowed from Cooper's grandmother's neighbor. The house was under construction; several exterior walls had been torn down and replaced with blue tarps flapping in the wind. From the local supermarket we bought beer with fake IDs and sheets of temporary tattoos. In the morning, arms covered in anchors and gulls, Cooper read aloud from *Billy Budd* while we drove back to New York. I tell you this to illustrate our immaturity. There is no version of this story in which Dan and I were never teenagers, never ridiculous. We were not uniquely prepared to know what we wanted.

Over Zoom, I ask you, "Did it freak you out?"

You say, "It really didn't."

And yet, I regretted sitting beside you at my wedding reception. Anxiety tightened your voice and radiated from the creases of your shimmery blue dress. Dan and I had exchanged vows beneath the St. John's Bridge in 95-degree heat. Sweating through dress shirts and sundresses, our guests—including Nana, Papa, Dan's grandparents, and LaVerne herself—carpooled to Mother's Bistro on SW 3rd Avenue in downtown Portland.

I was leaning across the table to talk to my friend Alix when you poked my shoulder. "Is there a menu? Is there a salad course?"

I look back on this year of my life with bewilderment. There are gaps in my memory. Dan and I got engaged in June 2009. We both graduated from our respective colleges that fall, a full semester early. He left Northfield, Minnesota and finally moved in with me in Portland. We rented a one-bedroom apartment at NW 21st and Lovejoy for seven hundred dollars a month. The recession was in full swing: Dan worked as an office temp and a census taker. I edited a friend's uncle's four-hundred-page fantasy novel and was rejected for a minimum wage position at a dog kennel. I gained twenty pounds. Dan got into PhD programs at Duke, Chicago, Georgetown, Boston College, and the University of Toronto—with an irreverent application he now refers to as "legitimately bonkers." In planning our wedding and the rest of our lives, we resisted interference, guidance. Dan's parents didn't want us to get married; you didn't want us to leave Portland. I don't remember making these decisions lightly—I don't remember making them at all. I had loved Dan since I was fifteen. Getting out of Oregon had always been my goal.

Maybe it wasn't until the wedding reception, at the table with my brand-new in-laws, that you realized the absence of a salad course reflected badly on you. There was a way in which this was all your fault.

A decade later, I ask you, "Did it freak you out when I got married really young?"

"It really didn't. I trusted you."

You trusted me, the way you're trusting me to write this book.

*

I take Wes to the beach—or what passes for the beach in Connecticut. It's November, and he does not ask permission to throw his shoes into the sand, or to strip down to his underwear and wade into the Long Island Sound. I sit on a damp rock and wait for him to get cold. There are towels in the car. Joggers, walkers, other mothers witness my child kicking at the waves. They crack jokes about global warming, social distance. A stranger's laughter is meant to point out the wrongness of my parenting, as well as the stranger's generous excusal of it. I know that.

How can I help letting Wes do exactly what he wants? Your trust in me—which I did nothing to deserve—made possible the best events of my life.

*

You have been trying to decide what to do about Nana. My grandma, your mother-in-law. Widowed in July, it's become hard for her to live independently. The decent nursing homes nearby are unaffordable. You would move her into your house, but the stairs are a problem. Your choices are to build a bedroom and bathroom onto the ground floor, or to move. But Portland has gotten expensive; after all these years, you would have to leave.

Dan and I also need to make a decision. He's been invited to teach the summer term at Deep Springs College, a school of thirty students in a remote valley in eastern California. It's a dream of his to be involved in this experimental school, where the students labor on a cattle ranch, practice self-governance, and isolate themselves deep in the desert. If we go, we'll give up childcare for half a year to drive cross-country and back with a four-year-old who frays our nerves on his best days. We might miss our chance to get vaccinated at Yale. And we'll risk getting sick on the road, uncovered by insurance—or at Deep Springs, thirty mountainous miles from a county hospital.

Saying yes to Deep Springs would mean packing our car to capacity and driving for days. Showing Wes the West: the alpine meadows of Colorado and arches of Moab and eerie skies over Nevada. Upon arriving in the valley, the dog could bound from the car and stay unleashed all summer. And when the term ends, we could drive to Oregon. After almost two years, we could be with you.

We want it both ways. A summer of work and stability, a sustainable routine. And also to blow it all up for a handful of life-defining moments. Choosing one will not make us want the alternative any less.

For now, we don't choose anything, and neither do you.

1978

In the spring she moves to Salt Lake City to finish nursing school. She lives alone in a studio whose single window overlooks a long residential road. If she leans out the window and cranes her neck, she can see the snow-capped summit of Mt. Wire. It's the bishop, not her fiancé, to whom she repents, confessing her cigarettes and occasional drinks. Her premarital sex with Casey. It's the bishop's job to set the price of forgiveness, and he demands a do-over: a gloriously sinless summer to prepare her for eternal marriage. Then she can have her "temple recommend."

Ellen does as the bishop says. She starts clinicals, working night shifts in the ED in Cottonwood. When their days off align, she and William swim laps in parallel lanes. She's a good swimmer. Her long torso slices through the water, her fingers extended in search of the pool's solid edge. The closest she and William come to intimacy is holding hands leaving the gym, hair wet and chlorinated. They talk about the future—or rather, William talks about his future. His ambitions: med school and fatherhood. He's dying to have "a whole bunch of kids." Ellen agrees without committing to a timeline—without telling him she's been on the pill for years, and has no intention of quitting.

By the fall, her purity has been restored: the church approves her and William for a temple wedding. On weekends she goes home with him to Idaho Falls, where it's his mother, not her own, helping her sew her wedding dress. Not the regulation temple gown she'll be required to wear for the endowment, but the dress she considers her real dress, for the reception at William's house.

She's alone in Salt Lake one night, half watching *M*A*S*H* and heating up chicken noodle soup, when someone knocks on the door. A familiar voice calls her name from the hall. She was never supposed to see him again.

Stooped in the doorframe, he says, "Don't do it."

She always knew she would see Casey again.

Ellen performs exasperation, then concern. "Come in," she says, as if Casey is the one who needs saving and she the reluctant woman for the job. Steam rises from the copper pot on the stove. A commercial for Velveeta plays on the TV. It's a little embarrassing, this small apartment with her bed so close to the refrigerator. The can opener splayed beside the emptied can of soup. The silver cross on a chain around her neck.

"You're going to regret it," he says.

And it's a little pleasurable, this swell of confidence—which she never feels around William—as she assures Casey she knows what she's doing. She maintains a dispassionate authority even as he repeats, incredulous, "You're not a Mormon!" As if it's his job to authenticate her marriage. What does Casey know? How else does a girl become a Mormon if not by claiming she's one?

But now he's crying, which means she's crying. The soup boils and she cuts off the gas.

Casey wants to know if she loves William. His belief that she doesn't is obvious. Ellen loved Casey flying across desert skies, therefore she can't love William—sturdy, dependable William—down here on the ground.

"I'm crazy about him," she says. Which is the truth. Casey has been demoted to unwanted big brother, a chaperone at the school dance of her brand-new adulthood.

"Yeah? You feel good with him, like you did with me?"

She looks at the ceiling. "You were never serious about me. Maybe you wanted to be, but you weren't."

"Look, you don't have to choose me! You don't have to choose anyone. That's what I came here to tell you. You don't need him, you don't need the church, you don't need any of this shit."

When she doesn't agree, he veers into cruelty, claiming her husband will expect submission and silence. Like LaVerne, she'll end up depressed and deflated in some shabby kitchen, numb to the needs of her own children, a stranger to herself. Argument gives way to exhaustion. He hugs her goodbye and she holds onto his shoulder blades. She soaks up the intensity of his attention, sensing she might need it later on. Although she's not oblivious to the power she still has over him, she can feel it fading the longer she ignores his warnings.

By the time she sees him again, a year from now, her power will be reduced to nothing.

1978

The endowment ceremony is not designed to drive women from the church: it's only the culmination of their girlhood aspirations. It's only an illustration of the faith to which they have always belonged. The woman who will be William's wife is unfazed by the endowment ceremony—or else able to appear unfazed. And hasn't that always been the unspoken requirement of wives, mothers—an ability to appear unfazed?

In 1978, for the initiatory, a woman stands nude beneath a sheet of paper, which has a hole for her head but no sleeves or seams. A temple worker washes the woman of her generation's blood and particular sins, naming each part of her body touched with a damp rag: head, ears, eyes, nose, mouth, neck, shoulders, back, breasts, bowels, arms, hands, loins, legs, feet. So that now you can speak faithfully, bear burdens, shit often, replenish the earth, and never feel weak or faint. The process is repeated with oil, which pools in your clavicle and drips down the backs of your thighs. Temple workers place their hands on your head and pray for you. They present you with your garment, your special Mormon underwear, that punchline of your faith. Finally, you are no longer naked. As grateful as Eve to be clothed.

Another temple worker whispers a new name into your ear. No one but your husband will ever learn it. Upon your death, he will call the new name to usher you through the gates of heaven. (Your husband also has a secret name. It's none of your business.) In 1978, you may or may not know that every girl initiated into the temple on this date has been given the same name. Depending on your reverence for the ritual, how charmed you are by the idea of a secret between you and your betrothed, learning you are one of many Ruths may or may not be a gut punch.

After you are anointed and re-named, prepared to be your husband's post-life priestess, you sit and watch a long performance. It's part play, part lecture, and requires audience participation. The actors are temple workers, untrained in the arts, awkwardly intoning their way through creation, the garden, the fall. You know the narrative is a Brigham Young remix, but you can't list the exact ways it deviates from the Old Testament. The play goes on as Lucifer tests his power and is banished. Straight-spined in a metal folding chair, you are schooled on the law of the gospel as represented in the Book of Mormon, the rules of obedience and subservience, which have been repeated to you all your life. You are made to mime the penalties of transgression: in front of strangers, you demonstrate how you will slit your throat, rip out your tongue, cup your own entrails in your hands. You are given more temple clothes: a white gown, a green apron to mimic the modesty of fig leaves, a veil to drape over your face.

You are led from a room representing the telestial world (white upholstery and ornate light fixtures) into a room representing the terrestrial world (walls muraled with trees). Your own death and afterlife are explained to you. Depending on your earthly behavior, you will qualify for one of three kingdoms—or rather, one of two kingdoms. Because the third, the most luxurious and holy, is reserved for men. Suppose you are too sinful for either kingdom?

Eternal darkness instead.

Now comes the veil. In order to pass from the terrestrial

world into the celestial kingdom, you approach a curtain splitting the room in two. You align yourself with the Five Points of Fellowship—that is, five holes cut in the cloth, through which you press your body against an unseen temple worker (tonight, playing the part of *the Lord*). On opposite sides of the white veil, the two of you stand ankle to ankle, knee to knee, breast to breast. Your hand on her back; your mouth to her ear. You whisper your secret name. The Lord admits you to the other side, where the boy you have agreed to marry is waiting. Your mother is also there, plus one of your little brothers—the only two members of your family who passed their worthiness interviews. You are sobbing now, because Casey was right. William wants an obedient priestess, a queen bearing her infinite babies in sorrow, a sister willing to cut out her own tongue and who never minded a stranger's oil-slicked finger all over her.

A woman who isn't completely creeped out right now.

He has the wrong girl. But there's no off-ramp. You might not remember this, but in the beginning you had a chance to bail. That first officiant gave you an out, and you—not yet violated, still more fearful of excommunication than of this marriage—neglected to raise your hand.

LaVerne, in her white robe and green apron, who has so rarely smiled at you, is beaming with pride. No one asks why you're crying so hard you're shaking. And now you are married, not only in this world, but in the next, and the next, and through the darkness surrounding it all.

*

I realize that all religions have their costumes, their ceremonies, their rituals, even their antiquated vows. I realize it's unfair to speak of a religion I do not practice—have never in my life practiced—with contempt and derision. But I'm not writing about the Mormon church; I'm writing about you. I am interested in the church only insofar as it touched my mother's life. And the truth is that it fucked you up.

*

The last church service I attended was Christmas Eve 2006. A year earlier I had dropped out of high school and now Dan was visiting. He and I would spend the week between Christmas and New Year's wandering downtown, ordering Thai noodles from food carts, driving to the coast and refusing to sleep until we were delirious with deprivation, laughing hard at a beetle crawling across a motel room's cracked ceiling. But first, at your request, I brought him to church.

It was the community church in which I'd been raised, attending Sunday school and Bible camp and singing in the youth choir. In the spirit of West Coast ambiguity, the church admitted to no domination and avoided the word *evangelical*, lest it be associated with the big-haired televangelists of the era. By 2006, the church, through a series of renovations and additions, had morphed into a mega church. Christmas Eve service was held in a stadium that seated several thousand people, and what transpired on stage was projected onto massive screens, across which scrolled psalms and lyrics and JESUS SAVES.

I was seventeen. Dan was eighteen. I don't remember if he tried to talk me out of it. I don't remember what we said to each other as we walked across the massive parking lot, through the cold rain and the main doors, where we accepted programs from a teenage usher. I remember you had saved us seats but were too far down the aisle to get up. You waved, your expression strained, as it often was back then. Probably in response to all three of your children, who were always quitting school, renouncing God, getting married or into car accidents.

The bulk of the service concerned neither Mary nor her tender-mild-holy infant, but the testimony of a local Portland man who had recently driven through the hills with a gun in his glove compartment, wanting to end it all. The sign for our church rose from the mist, stalwart and glowing. He wandered inside, sobbing, clutching his head in agony (on stage, and multiplied on screen, he demonstrated). He confessed the gun, the sinful ideation. He'd lost his job, his wife. His kids had stopped returning his calls. The guy had nothing to live for. But what he learned from Pastor Jeff was Jesus still loved him. And now he was here, on Christmas Eve—coincidentally the one night per year when the church was packed with new customers—to vouch for Jeff's ministry. And now the tithing baskets made their way down the aisle.

I was embarrassed to have subjected Dan to all this. Still, I hoped, when we got back in the car he would put his hand on my leg and tell me not to sweat it. Going to church once a year to appease my parents was no big deal.

Except, to him, it was. His unsparing review of the experience unleashed all the mortification and shame I had tried to suppress. Later, in the living room of the house on Troon Drive, deep into a number of wine bottles that would have scandalized other, less pious parents, I bitched about the service. Wasn't it tacky and crass? Practically a commercial! On Christmas! Andy and Pat both shrugged, citing the church's need to make money. They were open to the possibility that a genuinely suicidal man had been genuinely comforted by Pastor Jeff.

Dad came close to agreeing with me, wondering if you should seek out a smaller congregation.

You would not look at me. You rolled your eyes toward your

chardonnay. "I'm sorry you were traumatized by going to church with us *one time*. I'm sorry it's been so *painful* for you."

Of course, I had nothing to prove to you, who I expected would always believe in God, would always go easy on the imperfect institutions that brought you closer to your faith. The rant was for my boyfriend—though it didn't satisfy him. Dan and I ended the night in my apartment where I apologized, again, for taking him to church.

"It wasn't like that when I was growing up," I said. "It was just a regular church. There were no infomercials for Christ."

"All churches are bad," Dan said. "I'm not sure it makes any difference."

He told me it was freeing to stop believing in God. That God was for idiots—people too cowardly to face the truth about death, or to try to live a good life in the face of it.

"Are you calling me an idiot?" I asked.

"No," he said. "I know *you're* smarter than that."

We were teenagers. In our attempts to know ourselves, and to assert those selves, we could be cruel to each other. I shut myself into the bathroom, sat with my back against the clawfoot tub and cried. Within four years, we would be married beneath the St. John's Bridge by a judge we'd never met. "Was it a religious thing?" people would ask me afterward.

"No," I would claim. "The opposite."

*

We are at Dan's parents' house in Westchester. Wes has been on vacation from preschool for a week; all three of us were tested for Covid before we drove from New Haven to New York. That we received our negative test results on Christmas is a coincidence; the date, for Dan's family, is mostly a day off work.

You text me from the hospital: *Vaccinating my staff today!*

I'm on the verge of tears, drifting between the basketball games on TV, the spotless kitchen, the room where Wes is rowdily playing monster trucks with his grandpa. Annoyed with me, Dan tells me to get a snack. I don't want a snack; I want something beyond the walls of his childhood home, beyond the tri-state area and the restrictions of this year.

No one in our family went to church last night. No one will go this morning. These days, I'm not sure who believes in what. The reasons I haven't seen you in over a year have nothing to do with God—and yet, at age thirty-one, I find myself thinking, *I could go to church.* If you asked me to, I could sit through a service; I could rise and mouth the words to half-remembered songs. It wouldn't cost me anything.

I'm scared to ask if you and William slept together before you got married, but I ask. You say no, it was his first time and you pretended it was yours. "It was a terrible thing. I didn't want to do it. I was a liar, I was lying to him."

You mention you were on your period.

"You had your period throughout this whole day at the temple? You're not even supposed to be menstruating at the temple." In the recording, I sound proud of my research, my Latter-day Saints trivia. "It's not allowed!"

You roll your eyes. "Well, I was. And I remember…oh, God. You can't put any of this in the book. We went swimming first. Which is weird, don't you think? But then we went back to my apartment. I had this beautiful quilt somebody had made for me. I think maybe my mom had made it for me. But it was made out of really fragile fabric. This really thin, cottony material. Anyway, it got destroyed. And I could never clean it up. And I just remember that night was terrible. It was the worst night of my life."

"It sounds really hard," I say. "It sounds really sad."

What I don't say: *I am on your side. I don't give a fuck that you lied. This was everyone's fault but yours.*

You take a deep breath. "I don't know how you can make a story out of this. Honestly, Emily, it's just a sad story."

1978

For their honeymoon they drive to Manzanita, a small town on the Oregon coast. The cabin William borrowed from a friend of a friend is damp and cramped and full of mold. Each room contains more damaged furniture than it can comfortably hold; squeezing between couches, chairs, and scratched end tables is like navigating a storage unit. That night, when they pull the cheap cotton covers to their shoulders, sparks crackle and fly. In the morning William goes to the bathroom and returns ten minutes later, something small and plastic cupped in his hand.

Ellen is belly-down on the unmade bed, writing in her journal. She's not immediately curious. Not until William lifts the receiver of a brown rotary phone and dials the number printed on her circular case of pills.

"What are you doing?"

That she sounds more incredulous than ashamed is not a point in her favor.

He raises a finger. Polite, even now. A good Mormon boy does not recognize the distinctive packaging of oral contraceptives. A good Mormon boy telephones his wife's doctor for answers, apparently.

Ellen sits up on the bed and watches this performance. He could have asked her. Better yet, he could have left her toiletries zipped into their opaque travel case. Is she seeing him clearly for the first time? Her husband nods, taking in the confidential information Ellen's doctor in Utah offers him freely.

"Who are you?" William asks, hanging up. "Who did I marry?"

All her life, she's been prone to fast tears. The *waterworks*, her brothers would say. She's frantic now, her tongue tripping over a practical explanation: she takes the pills to regulate her periods. If she doesn't take them, her cramps are so bad; she has thrown up from the pain, she swears. Shouldn't William, future Dr. Strout, accept this answer?

Outside, the ocean roars and laps at cold sand. Inside, the lamplight is the color of a fever. Fleetingly, she wants her mom. Then Casey. Then no one.

William sinks into a faded chintz chair. He picks at the stuffing emerging from one armrest. For a moment, Ellen thinks maybe he'll let it go. The sun will rise over Highway 101 and they'll eat bread bowls of clam chowder at a picnic table.

"Were you a virgin when I met you?" he asks.

The sum of what he knows about her is already almost too much. After they got engaged, she presented him with a number of possible deal-breakers: her Jack Mormon father. Her clove cigarettes. The two engagement rings she has already worn and returned. He accepted these flaws gracefully, which was satisfying for both of them. William got to think of himself as progressive, forgiving, unafraid of the truth. And Ellen allowed herself the luxurious assumption that if William had remained at her side after everything she'd told him, there was nothing that could make him leave.

"I confessed to the bishop. And he said I was forgiven."

William laughs at her. "Forgiven by who?"

*

Maybe you remember this.

I was a teenager, but young, fourteen at the most. You and I drove to the coast for the day. It's possible we visited LaVerne, who was by then living in your little brother's basement in Newport. Possible, but not likely, because we rarely visited LaVerne. Growing up, I saw your mother no more than once a year. After

I left home, I saw her twice before she died. Then again, I do remember you were rattled and restless—the mood that, at home, would have compelled you to rearrange the furniture.

"Should we try to find a room for the night?" You were behind the wheel of your Volkswagen Beetle, the last manual car you owned, whose clutch I would burn through a year later.

I agreed. We were driving through one of the coastal towns still untouched by money. Netarts, or Ocean City. We pulled up to a two-story motel with an illuminated VACANCY sign. The woman behind the front desk had a commotion of frizzed gray hair and a shapeless floral button-down, the kind of polyester blouse I associated with LaVerne. "Problem is," she told us, "none of the rooms have been cleaned yet. But I can show you what we got, and if you come back at three we'll get you checked in."

Why would a motel manager show off the mess of a recently vacated room? Why did she unlock the door and present to us the wreck of the unmade bed, the tangle of wet towels soaking the carpet, the takeout containers piled atop the nightstand, the red Gideon's Bible on the floor? Sun-faded curtains, heavy with dust, shifted in front of the open window.

"Thanks," you said, reversing out of the room. "Let me think about it."

Back in the car, you said, "We have to get out of here."

I shrugged, disappointed if only because I worried the day would end with us with driving back to Portland—and confused but not overly curious about the wild look in your eyes.

We drove to Cannon Beach, the most expensive of the tourist towns, and rented a suite for three times the cost of the uncleaned room.

"Much better." You were cheerful, yourself again. "That other place gave me the creeps."

*

The year I was fourteen was also the year you told me about your first husband. We were camping on Mt. Hood. You built a fire. We sat with our backs against a log and you told me you'd made a lot of youthful mistakes concerning who to love and, eventually, who to marry. You also told me you and William had realized your error in the hours following the temple ceremony, and that your marriage was quickly annulled.

I'm surprised, late in the fall of 2020, to learn your first marriage lasted closer to a year. Over Zoom, you describe the apartment you rented, the psychiatrist William made you see, as if a doctor could erase your past. William was studying for the MCATs. You were finishing nursing school.

"Wait," I say in the recording. My confusion is high pitched as I register the lie. "How long were you guys married?"

William did convince the church to declare your union null and void. But legally, your only option was to file for divorce.

If I hadn't asked, I would never have known.

1979

It is fall again when Ellen shows up at her parents' farmhouse in Ontario, crying and unannounced. LaVerne answers the door, face arranged into her signature mask of incredulity verging on disgust. "What's the matter with you?" she asks, a can of pop sweating in her hand.

Ellen moves inside and sinks into one corner of the couch. She clutches her knees. "I don't know. He left. He said he was done and he left."

Ellen's little sister lies across a braided rug in front of a fireplace no one has ever swept. She kicks her bare feet as she reads a Nancy Drew book. Normally Elizabeth would launch herself into her sister's arms, but today she seems shy and detached. The boys are upstairs, pacing their bedrooms, waiting for their dad to take them pheasant hunting.

"What did you do?" LaVerne demands.

"I didn't do anything," Ellen insists, knowing it's the truth, and that another version of the truth would be: *everything*.

Earl Sr. appears in the doorframe, in his camouflage cap and orange jacket. "Why's she here? Why's she crying like that?"

"She went and broke up with William," LaVerne explains.

Ellen's shoulders shake. She cries harder each time someone comments on her crying. Abruptly, her dad tells her to get in the truck.

The boys shout their protests down the stairs.

"I'm taking your sister this time," Earl bellows back at them. "And I don't want to hear another word about it."

It's October and the grass has lost its color, but as the sun goes down it sets the pale fields ablaze. The 12-gauge is both lighter and more awkward than Ellen expected it to be. Her father is nearly a stranger, and this will be near to her last memory of him.

"Aim for the tailfeathers," he says. "Swing your barrel through the body of the bird."

A pheasant, disrupted by her dad's spaniel, bursts from the grass and into the air. Ellen does her best to follow instructions: she squeezes the trigger and her heart rate spikes and the bird, with its auburn chest and black-spotted wings, flies away.

*

In our interviews, I keep using the word *aspiration* when discussing your effort to find a husband. You correct me every time. "I wouldn't say I *aspired* to any of this. It was what was expected of me."

It takes me months to understand the difference. It wasn't that you clung to a vision of perfect Mormon domesticity. Eight kids, two ovens, view of the Wasatch Range: that was never your fantasy. What you wanted, in any given moment, was to be loved unconditionally. By your mother. Your brothers. By a man who would choose you and stay with you, whose own family would accept you.

Those were your aspirations, and a marriage to a Mormon man sanctioned by the Mormon church was the way forward. Sure, you could have married Casey—except LaVerne would not have forgiven you, and Casey, with his Cessna and wanderlust and casual girlfriends, was a literal flight risk.

That wedding in the temple, those white robes and green aprons, was billed as the path of least resistance. That the path turned out to be covered in snakes and loose rock must have been heartbreaking. That your map offered no alternative, more so.

In January 2021, Wes finally learns to wear a coat, then a snowsuit. One night we take his sled to the hill behind the Yale Divinity School; I dig my boots into the snow to prevent us from crashing into a wrought iron fence. As we skid to a stop, Wes points at the sky and says, "Look at the beautiful moon."

I look at the beautiful moon and start to see it—how a person could live her life here.

Dan and I spend more time together than we have since Wes was born. We write through the mornings at our scratched kitchen table and run increasingly fast miles at the abandoned high school track, sweat freezing at our temples. We hike with the dog in West Rock Ridge State Park, memorizing the twists and forks of the trails. We have sex at odd midday hours while Wes is at school, and in those moments I regret nothing—not the unwashed dishes, or the credit card debt, or the ever-changing zip code.

Our upstairs neighbor, a medical resident, asks if I can walk his dog halfway through his sixteen-hour shifts. Predictably, I fall in love with his fawn-colored pit bull, and Zoey's daily walk becomes a fulltime residency on our couch. Connecticut will never be home, but our Wocster Square apartment, full of dogs and books and Matchbox cars, is starting to feel close.

One afternoon, Dan and I look at each other with the same

realization. We should stay, shouldn't we? We should not pull our son out of school and drive 3,500 miles to live in the desert without childcare. We might want to be the versions of ourselves who wanted that, but we're not anymore. For once, we'll choose stability. For once, we will go an entire summer without packing up the car.

We've made our choice.

When Dan delays calling Deep Springs to officially turn down their offer, I don't say a word.

1979

After her divorce she calls Casey for the first time in a year. She is crying as she dials his number, long memorized, and she's still crying when he picks up. She tries to say, "It's me," and can't get the words out.

He says, "If only we could have seen this coming."

Her sobs veer into laughter.

"Aisle or window seat?" he asks.

She goes to Chicago. She sleeps on his couch. They spend a week driving around the Midwest: to Lake Geneva in Wisconsin; to Saugatuck in Michigan; to Starved Rock State Park in Illinois. When he grabs her hand above the gearshift, she holds on tight.

Standing on a dock above some cold expanse of water, he kisses her hairline. She knows Casey is only fulfilling a vow he made a year ago: to pick up the pieces. She will fly home to Utah and never see him again. She's grateful to him, even so.

A month later she moves from Salt Lake City back to Provo for a job in an Immediate Care Unit. No longer a Mormon, she makes new friends. She goes to parties, smokes, drinks. In dark bars she meets twentysomethings who made Utah their home after escaping treatment centers for troubled youths. The state's combination of wilderness, holiness, and lawlessness is perfect for "rehabilitating" badly behaved teens. It's easy for Ellen to imagine another life, one in which her parents predict her future and desperately try to thwart it.

Instead, she went to Ricks College and BYU. She married the good Mormon boy when he asked. And still she is drunk in the glow of a Budweiser sign, sawdust beneath her shoes, wondering if she'll speak to her mother again.

*

"Did you ever think about—" This question is important, and in the recording I stumble over my words. "When you left William, and you left the Mormon church, did you ever think about giving up religion altogether?"

"No," you say automatically. "It's interesting that you ask that. Faith was still important to me. I couldn't discard it, I just had to find a different avenue for it. It isn't until now that I'm questioning everything. Back then, I needed that context just to…keep going. And now I'm not sure if that context works for me anymore."

I'm silent, not wanting to spook you. You have said something I thought I would never hear you say.

You say, "I want it—I really want it to. But it just doesn't seem to work anymore."

*

Between 1979 and 1981, you dove from Mormonism into evangelical Christianity. Why did you, in your early twenties, need religion? And why did I not?

93

Even before a Christmas Eve service mortified me in front of my boyfriend, God had lost his hold on me, or I had let go. There were times when I wanted my childhood faith back, if only as an insurance policy. The hardest part was abandoning my belief that nothing very bad would ever happen to me. (If this seems like a juvenile experience of faith, it's because I lost mine young.) Outside of a desire to be pre-approved for good luck, nothing about prayer, worship, or evangelizing appealed to me. I was fine with church-bred conservative politics until I wasn't—until friends came out to me, until I started having sex, until I considered unwanted pregnancy. Like you, I am prone to tears; my voice thickens when I talk about childbirth, basketball, certain mountain ranges. Unlike you, a sermon never made me weep

At fifteen, when I was still ambivalently attending youth group on Wednesday nights, wishing I found religion half as satisfying as Raymond Carver stories or making out, I would have given anything to hear you express doubt in God. In February 2021, over Zoom, you describe a breach in your lifelong faith and I feel sad. Why? Did your piety give me permission to shrug off religion? You used to speculate that if you died before your mother, LaVerne would pray over your body, pleading for your admittance to the kingdom. LaVerne kneeling beside your corpse was an illustration of her love for you—as well as her rejection of you. Have I been counting on you to do the same for me?

Or maybe it scares me—the extent to which you have allowed yourself to change. The number of things I thought I'd never hear you say.

Also at fifteen, I was desperate to fall in love. I looked for it on the internet, in the smirk of every boy whose hand grazed mine. What if it hadn't been Dan who loved me back, but someone who also loved Jesus? Would I not have let religion sink its teeth into me?

Later, when I desperately wanted you to be exactly who you were except more progressive, more irreverent, less Oregon, less 1970s, and you said, scornfully, "Believe me, you're never going to abort Dan's baby," I thought you were probably right. Now, I think you may have been trying to say something else, and in your attempt, projecting a belief system onto Dan that never applied to him.

If you meant I would do anything to keep his love—would follow him to any country, church, or altar—then yes, I would have. At least that far.

1980

Three months after the eruption of Mount St. Helens, she leaves Utah for good. Her oldest brother James is finishing his residency at a hospital in Portland; he and his wife, high school sweethearts, invite Ellen to move into their apartment downtown until she finds a job.

Ellen drives past Ontario without stopping to see her parents or the twins. She drives west until the highway hugs the Columbia River and the hills are steep and timbered.

Everyone has the landscape that looks correct to them, that signals *home* to their mind. For her, it's Hood looming above the gorge. The red cliffs guarding the wide river. She tells herself she will never leave Portland again, will spend her life trying to discern, through clouds, the outlines of mountains she can name.

*

In 2015, you were crossing the glass-enclosed pedestrian bridge that connects OHSU to the Veterans Hospital, admiring the view of the Willamette Valley, when a man said your name. Because time had not touched your thick hair or high cheekbones—and because every Oregonian makes their way to this particular hospital, eventually—you were used to being recognized. To facing, mid-shift, the occasional ghost. With calm curiosity, you turned toward the voice.

The bald, white-stubbled man was a stranger.

"Excuse me?" you said.

He narrowed his eyes. "I'm sure that's you."

The eyes were the same.

"Oh my god," you said in a rush of recognition. "William."

The two of you had coffee in the cafeteria. You suppressed an urge to joke about him drinking caffeine, the devil's refreshment. William was a neurosurgeon, in town for a conference, and no longer a Mormon. Since your wedding in the Salt Lake Temple, he'd been married twice more. He mentioned he called LaVerne after you split up. He tried several times, but she wouldn't give him your contact information.

"Are you serious?" you said. "God, I would have loved to have heard from you."

Mostly you talked about your children. William had five, the first three of similar ages to Andy, Pat, and me. Your ex-husband was warm and kind, but he made no direct reference to what had happened between you. There was no apology. He drained his coffee and left in a hurry, late for a presentation.

On October 15, 2019, William committed suicide. His sister called you and told you the news. "I don't know if you kept in touch," she said, "but I thought it might be important for you to know." You were shocked, and grateful to her for calling.

Two years later, over Zoom, you tell me, "He was only sixty-four. I have a hard time with that. It makes me feel really bad."

Your eyes drift toward your bedroom ceiling. The present collapses into the past. I'm used to it now; I've stopped trying to control the conversation. My job is to fling open doors and let you choose which one to walk through.

"I remember at the time not understanding why we couldn't…. I thought that we loved each other! I couldn't understand it. It was really devastating that he couldn't forgive me for being a stupid kid."

*

I spend a morning searching for information about William's life and death. I learn he loved his children unconditionally; that his Mormon parents raised him to have strong morals; that he enjoyed the outdoors, dancing, and the color brown. On a memorial page, his widow describes his cause of death as "parental alienation." She believes he killed himself because his ex-wife, in cooperation with the legal system, kept him from his biological children.

I could impose a narrative on William's life, a narrative about fatherhood. He married you because he wanted to have "a bunch of kids." Later, he ended his life because he lost custody of his children. But I don't know what kind of father William was. I don't know the specific turmoil of his sixty-four years.

I find a picture of him in Salt Lake City, 1975, taken as he enters the mission home where he'll spend a few days preparing for his trip to El Salvador. In the picture, his hair is cut straight across his forehead. He squints through frameless glasses. Suit, tie, wool overcoat. A leather satchel over one shoulder, a suitcase in the opposite hand. Snow melts on the ground. William's mouth hangs open.

In the picture he is fresh from his own initiation, that day-long temple ritual about which he will, years later, decline to warn you.

You are not mentioned in his obituary.

On February 23, 2021, Wes hits a little girl at school. One of his teachers, Sharon, informs Dan at pick-up. In a rush to get home, Dan confirms the girl is okay, that Wes apologized, and the rest of the day passed without incident.

"But we'd like to schedule a time to speak to you and Emily," Sharon adds. "Just about Wesley's behavior in general."

Dan texts me while I'm waiting in line at the grocery store. My heart breaks, but it's a poignant kind of heartbreak. I didn't see Wes hit his friend; I can't explain what upset him, or what he was thinking. That Wes and I are apart seven hours a day renders Wes, improbably, separate from me. The novelty of this new phase of motherhood almost overshadows my anxiety.

Two nights later, after putting our son to bed, we meet with Wes's teachers Sharon and Maggie over Zoom. It's strange to see one another unmasked. The teachers greet us wearily, their faces creased with exaggerated concern. They have already decided how this conversation will end.

Wes hit a little girl, yes, but he also flings sand at other children and giggles. Instead of cooperating with his classmates' age-appropriate imaginative play, he bumps into them. Taps their shoulders. Upends their block towers. The teachers compare him, unfavorably, to a kid a full year older than Wes, the son of a biostatistics professor, who recently regaled the class with facts about the Mars Rover.

Wes is incapable of waiting in line to wash his hands. Of napping at naptime. Of staying on his carpet square for "meeting time" or filling an entire pegboard with colored pegs. He teases his teachers; he pretends to pour water on them. They cry "No!" and he laughs and does it again. He makes frequent, repetitive "big noises" when he should be "turning his voice off."

With irritation barely obscured by the grain of the video call, Maggie—who teaches the kids yoga and wears handknit scarves— shudders and says, "Wesley is *not* feeling peaceful in his body."

Having presented their evidence, the teachers tell us, again, to have Wes evaluated. They are almost comically careful to avoid saying the word *autism*, even as they paint Wes in autistic clichés. I understand they are not doctors, and that for them to invoke their suspected diagnosis would be unprofessional. Equally unprofessional, I think, is their apparent certainty that a diagnosis is inevitable and will justify their complaints, their frustration with Wesley's many *behaviors*.

Later, I will say to Dan, "If Wes is on the spectrum, won't that make their treatment of him worse, not better?"

Over the next week, I frantically try to prevent my kid from flunking out of ivy league preschool. I send him to school with my old iPod and a pair of headphones, and I show his teachers how to queue up a playlist of Wes's favorite Big Thief songs, guaranteed to keep him quiet for an hour at naptime. I pay attention to my interactions with Wes at home, the subconscious methods with which he has trained me to parent him. Yelling "no" does not work; he interprets it as a dare. Ignoring him does not work; he would burn down the house for a moment of eye contact. He needs redirection, and for me to acknowledge his emotions as facts, not emergencies: *You're angry because you're not allowed to ride your bike inside. You're sad because it rains every day.*

And: *I am also angry. I am also sad.*

I explain all of this in an email to my son's teachers, expecting them to care, even to thank me for trying to help. Maggie responds: *It sounds like some of the behaviors we are seeing at school are also showing themselves at home.*

At home, Wes is rambunctious and stubborn, curious and ravenous for attention. He is wildly smart—a walking catalog of street names, highway exits, towns he has lived in, people he has met. He remembers every book we've ever read to him and can sing the chorus of any song he's heard twice. He likes to put his hands on animals, to inform strangers he will soon be four. What he needs is to be outside, moving his body and breathing fresh air. What he resents is a small room, a pointless task. For Wes, hell is a jigsaw puzzle.

I will admit he is difficult; three-year-olds can be difficult. And his development is delayed: he began speaking in full sentences well after his second birthday. He still struggles with utensils, crayons, and dressing himself. Part of me wants badly to trust the judgement of the teachers with whom I've left Wes most mornings since September. It's the teachers who enabled all those hikes with my husband, the hours I've spent writing this book. More than anything, I want to do right by my kid, which probably means taking seriously his *behaviors*, several of which the internet lists as "potential red flags."

Still, watching him bang on bongo drums, or sing to his stuffed animals, or career across a playground, the same question keeps nagging at me. Should a three-year-old really be required to "turn off his voice" or "feel peaceful in his body"?

Does the preschool teacher shuddering over Zoom feel peaceful in hers?

*

On March 8th, Dan and I go to Stop & Shop for cake ingredients. Wes's birthday is in two days. Dan asks for my opinion on sprinkles, but I'm distracted by an email from Sharon.

Subject line: "Observations of Wes During Mealtimes."

The email—written in stilted legalese—reports that Wes "shoves entire strawberry halves into his mouth, rather than taking bites." Indeed, his teachers are so worried about him choking they brought in a nurse consultant—without telling Dan or me—to observe him scarfing his berries. The nurse also caught Wes "hopping out of his seat" and "making big sounds." Because Wes requires constant supervision while he eats, lest he choke, Wes's presence poses a safety risk for the other children— who, unsupervised, might choke. For now, Wes will eat lunch alone in Sharon's office. She ends the email by instructing me to ask Yale Child Study Center to send her copies of the evaluation forms they sent us.

Heart racing in the baking aisle, I hand my phone to Dan and say, "He's getting kicked out of school."

Dan reads the email and we look at each other in disbelief. It's not that any particular "observation" is a shock to us. But the speed at which his preschool experience has gone to shit activates a kind of mania to which I am hopelessly prone, and to which Dan has never been immune. I want to fix this. I want to be living through a different moment in my life.

In the car, Dan throws his head against the seatback. "I need to voice a selfish thought."

I wait.

"I have this vision of us stuck in Connecticut with no childcare all summer. And we'll wish we had gone to Deep Springs."

I laugh. The same way I laughed when you told me I could drop out of high school. The way I laughed when I called my friend Kirstin from New York, summer of 2005, and she told me, "Don't fall in love with him." The sun beats on the windshield and melts the snow at the edges of the parking lot. Hope blooms in my chest and I almost give into it—but how can I? I'm Wes's mother. The teachers to whom I pay seven hundred dollars a month to ensure he's okay are telling me he's not.

"We have to stay," I decide. "We have to get him whatever help he needs."

*

Later that night, when Wes is asleep, I forward "Observations of Wes During Mealtimes" to my friend.

My first reaction, she tells me, *is I hate these people. And while "the behaviors" is a rich phrase from a novelistic point of view, it's a vague and meaningless concept here. He eats half a strawberry at once? Oh, how monstrous!*

She sends me a video of her nine-year-old stuffing most of a burrito into his mouth.

*

We are all sick. For two days, including his fourth birthday, Wes stays home from school. He gets a keyboard, a chocolate cake, a Covid test. After blowing out his candles, he pounds the table for emphasis. "I'm four now," he says, reaching for the cake. Then, catching himself: "I gotta get a spoon."

On March 11th, I pick him up from preschool. Sharon meets me outside and her voice cracks on the edge of hysteria as she tells me Wes pushed a plastic table into her legs. She wasn't hurt, but easily could have been. Worse, Wes could have injured another child. The teachers have tried everything: getting right down in his face and telling him *no*. Isolating him when his behavior bothers other children. Holding him in their laps during circle time. They never make him wait his turn anymore. The bathroom, the sink, the art supplies—he gets everything first.

As Sharon explains the hopelessness of the situation, Wes approaches with something hidden behind his back. He waits for his teacher to make eye contact before he flings a twig at her midsection.

"You see?" she says to me. "This is why we pushed for the evaluation."

I take him home. I ask him why he pushed a table into his teacher. He smirks and throws a shoe at me and I scream at my son until my throat is raw. I scream at Wes the way you never screamed at me.

After bedtime, Dan finally calls the dean at Deep Springs and tells her we're not coming—that our kid is having a hard time, there could be something wrong with him. We have to figure it out.

Wes never goes back to school.

Sometimes I can't believe I am raising a child without you.
Wes hasn't seen you since he was two. He remembers you, or
at least he holds you in his mind as a character: Grandma Ellen.
Over the phone you tell him, "I think I should come visit you
soon." He spends the next week asking when you'll be here.

You fear not being in his life. Being unknown to him. To
me, that seems as unlikely as you and I being unknown to each
other. But Wes will not always embrace Grandma as an abstract
concept, a visitor who's always on her way.

I want to drive him to your house. Park in the driveway.
Open the front door and let Wes and the dog enter in a burst
of unchecked energy. Even before a virus canceled all our plans,
this was a frequent fantasy. Because when I did see you, we had
to negotiate sleeping arrangements, jetlag, visits by siblings and
grandparents, dinners made or bought, gifts consequential or
frivolous, church services attended or skipped. What I want is
to call you spontaneously on a Sunday morning, to arrive before
the frost burns off. What I want is to take for granted your near-
ness, like I did for twenty-one years and not a day longer.

*

Your visits often coincide with emergencies. In 2017, your plane landed in Toronto as Wes's birth went awry. In 2019, you flew to Richmond in the days before we found out Dan had Rocky Mountain Spotted Fever. I believe in a version of myself that you'd like a lot better than the one you get. I suspect I'm capable of hospitality and generosity, of endless conversation, of relaxing with you. But when you're around, I'm almost always stressed— short on sleep and patience, withdrawn. Need—my need— forces you to book plane tickets. But there's no denying that for you I am my worst self.

At the end of March 2021, we see each other for the first time in over a year, one week after Dan and I have abruptly terminated our contract with Wes's daycare. In the interim, we've spoken with the public school district's special ed coordinator— along with their social worker, psychiatrist, and speech therapist—all of whom concluded Wes is fine. He doesn't even qualify for an evaluation through their system.

Since pulling him out of preschool, we have seen no trace of the behaviors that concerned Wes's teachers. His delayed speech has exploded into a ceaseless litany of questions, observations, memories of our years in Richmond, on which he never before had the skills to reflect: "Remember the cow in Virginia? We fed him grass. What was his name?" He's sleeping better, eating better. Sometimes I tell him, "Please don't do that," and he actually listens.

We bring him with us to pick you up from the airport. The two of you hug outside the terminal at JFK, eyes flashing joyfully above your masks.

There's traffic on 95, and the drive back to New Haven takes two hours. You and Wes sit together on the backseat. He calls you "Grandma Ellen" before settling on "Ellen" and you promise you don't mind. "There's absolutely nothing wrong with him," you tell me. Your tone is celebratory, but serrated, like you're ready to fight.

By the end of the week, you're less sure. Dan and I go for a walk by ourselves, leaving you and Wes alone together. He does well for an hour, then throws a book across the room. More books. A ukulele. A doll. You try to distract him with Legos and he scatters the pieces. As he did his teachers, he looks you in the eye. As at preschool, he's the only one laughing.

The Child Study Center sends me a questionnaire to fill out in advance of our long-anticipated appointment—which, in the spirit of parental due diligence, we've decided to keep. *Does your child act sillier than his peers? Do your child's moods shift suddenly, without warning? Does your child lose interest in activities too quickly? Does your child keep laughing after everyone else has stopped?*

I say goodbye to you outside your Airbnb. It's dark and the air smells like rain. I'm silent and stiff, dreading Wes's upcoming evaluation, fearing—as I suppose I have since he was in utero— a doctor's power to tell me something has gone wrong.

Families spill from Sally's Apizza, masks around their chins. A man pats the hood of his brother's truck and says, "You keeping the Ford?" Wearily, the brother says, "I'm keeping the Ford."

I'm wearing running shorts, though it's barely spring. Hank's leash is wrapped around my wrist twice. We hold each other, and one of us cries, infecting the other. I hate that this is how I show my love for you: sobbing on a street corner. I do it every time.

*

I wonder how I've disappointed you. If you worry about me, and if those two things are the same. Do you ever want to grab me by the shoulders and demand to know that I'm okay? If I acquiesced, if I screamed "I'm okay!" until my scream echoed across the Long Island Sound, would you be satisfied? Or would you still have doubts?

*

Only one of us can go with Wes to the evaluation, which will happen over four consecutive Tuesdays in March and April. Dan takes him to the first appointment, because I'm scared. All Wes knows is Grandma has left, he no longer attends school, and today he's going to Yale—where his dad works, where he sometimes rides his scooter and gets an ice cream cone—to talk to some doctors. He brings Dave, his stuffed dolphin, and introduces Dave to the graduate student tasked with the evaluation. Amelia's reaction is cordial, chilly. Colder still is the small, windowless room into which she leads Wes and Dan. A double mirror reflects white walls and fluorescent lights, a small table and chairs. Without further ado, Amelia administers what Dan will later describe as "the toddler SATs."

Can Wes duplicate Amelia's complex block tower? He cannot. Can Wes select two identical forms from a worksheet of anatomically detailed black-and-white sketches of insects—bees and grasshoppers and flies? He cannot.

He can get up from his chair, fling open a cabinet, and produce a toy school bus.

"You may play with that *after* you answer my questions," Amelia says.

Dan tries to split the difference. "Maybe he can play with it *while* he answers your questions."

Wes brings the bus back to the table. "What do you call a person who wears a crown?" Amelia asks, without preamble or inflection. Wes doesn't know. "What is the color of most dirt?" Wes guesses, "Black." "What is the name of your littlest finger?" Amelia keeps her own hands hidden in her lap.

Wes doesn't know the name of his littlest finger either because he has never asked or because we never thought to tell him. He starts to fuss and fidget. Does he think of school—his teachers' frustration at his inability to sit still and draw a person with four or more body parts? His indifference to hours upon hours of Magna-Tiles, peg boards, and smaller and larger cups?

Amelia says, "If you can't answer my questions, I need to take away the bus."

Wes says he's ready to go home.

Amelia pretends to pout. "You don't want to play with me?"

Wes locates the switch and turns off the lights.

*

Wes and I drive to the beach in East Haven where we last went with you. Remember the carousel in the boarded-up garage, the lighthouse? A coin-operated telescope inspired Wes to say, "Mom, can I have a quarter?" A question that, for reasons you'll remember, brought back my entire childhood.

This time, we park the car and get out and the ocean reminds Wes that you were here and now are gone. He cries. He doesn't want to put his feet in the water or dig in the sand. He doesn't care about the great big ships passing through the harbor.

I say, "We can have fun without Grandma, trust me."

Wes cries harder and I realize he doesn't. He has trusted me before and will probably trust me again—but not today. I carry him to a picnic table and let his tears slide down my neck. I want to know what you would do about this. About any of it.

*

A friend reads a draft of this book and wants to know how I felt about school as a kid. At first, I say I felt fine about it. Certainly

I was calm, obedient. Certainly I filled the peg boards with colored pegs when asked.

I was also remote, withdrawn. In first grade I learned to read and write quickly; it seemed the teacher had excavated those skills from my soul. Otherwise I was almost clinically incapable of listening to instructions and following them. I looked out windows, daydreamed, faked sick. I passed notes to my friends until they asked me to stop. In middle school I failed science because I had a crush on the kid assigned to sit next to me; the only thing I memorized was the way his hair curled into his left ear. My first year of high school I spent wandering the halls, hiding in stairwells, asking boys to drive me downtown. In tenth grade, a brief mania of academic ambition prompted me to ask for a math tutor, whom you hired willingly. I got straight A's for a semester and applied to the program in New York City where I would meet Dan, and after which I would come home and drop out of high school.

Does my "atypical" child come as a surprise?

Doesn't everyone come as a surprise, if you let them?

*

When Wes finds out we're going back to Yale for round two of his evaluation, he throws himself onto our bed wailing, trembling, resisting my effort to pry his body from a heap of pillows. But we are going to this appointment: I will stay calm and channel Ellen; Wes will absorb my confidence. This time, he will ace the toddler SATs. "There's nothing wrong with him," Amelia will be forced to admit, in spite of her research, before diagnosing his preschool teachers as mean bitches. Having gotten to the root of the problem, I'll share the good news with the family group chat. I'll find Wes a new school for next year. I'll get back to writing my book, in which the main character is you, not me, certainly not Wes gasping, gagging on his own saliva.

"We can get a cookie afterward," I plead. "The biggest cookie you've ever seen."

To invoke the record-breaking cookie is to admit defeat. It's Dan who lugs all forty pounds of our son from the mattress and says to me, "We're not doing this. He's not a lab rat."

Dan calls the Child Study Center and cancels the rest of our appointments. I pour Goldfish into a bowl and turn on *Clifford*. Dan is stomping around the apartment half naked, late for work, not pleased.

In pictures, the lush campus of Deep Springs is surrounded by miles of sand and sage, guarded by sun-bleached mountains. It has been months, nearly years, since I've seen Dad, Nana, Andy, Char, Micaela, Pat. The last time I was on the West Coast, Claire wasn't two and Papa wasn't dead. My nephew hadn't yet been born.

We thought we could choose stability over Deep Springs. In the absence of stability, we chose disaster. But what if our son—behaviors and all—isn't a disaster?

I know what you would tell me to do: finish the evaluation. Take the results with a grain of salt; Wes is still so young. Try a different preschool in the fall. Hang in there, talk soon! But I also know what you would actually do.

Dan's hand is on the door when I say, "Is it too late to call Deep Springs?"

He gives me the same look he gave me after our first kiss. Like I'm the bad news he was hoping for.

"Tell them we changed our minds," I say.

*

The dean is unsure she can swing it. The students have already signed up for their summer classes. Housing has already been assigned to visiting faculty. Maybe if enough kids agree to drop a course and take Dan's instead? And maybe if we're willing to move into Henderson Station, a house at the base of the mountains two miles from campus? *Advantages: it's large, private, has a great view. Disadvantages: it's not exactly an aesthetic gem: its kitchen is made up of parts of many other kitchens, and it has shag carpet, but it's serviceable!*

Dan reads this email aloud to me. Have I ever wanted anything as much as I want to disappear into the desert? The whole of my plan is to let Wes out the backdoor each morning and watch, not judge, what he does.

For two weeks, we get no answer. We live with the kind of anticipation I associate with an editor reading my manuscript. Then Dan checks his email as he's coming up the stairs to our apartment. Six kids have signed up for his Machiavelli course. According to Carla, the student in charge of the curriculum committee, six is plenty.

We leave in fifteen days and we'll be gone four months.

1981

Jazz De Opus, on NW Couch and 2nd, is supposed to be the Village Vanguard of Portland. Ellen has never been to New York: is the Vanguard also covered in dark wood paneling? Are clubs in Manhattan crowded with ferns and fire pits? She is cross-legged on a barstool waiting for her boyfriend's set when her sister-in-law, with whom she lived most of last year, says, "Hey, look, that's Bob Adrian."

The name jolts her memory. At Putnam High School, Bob Adrian was disheveled, grungy. His shoulder-length hair was dark and tangled. But the tall man weaving around velvet couches and potted plants is handsome, well-groomed. She likes his mustache. She has always liked a good mustache.

As he crosses the crowded club, his guitar case bumps into women half-reclined on bean bag chairs. These women have come with friends, combed their perms into manes and ordered Pina Coladas. All they want is to catch his eye—but Bob catches Ellen's eye and smiles without hesitation or embarrassment. It's clear he remembers her. People usually do.

Ellen's boyfriend Jimmy has a trust fund and expects to inherit his father's diamond shop. Jimmy believes he's a better musician than he is. He wants to marry Ellen, and her response so far has been *maybe? Someday?* As Bob takes the stage and begins to play "Autumn Leaves," she changes her mind. The answer is *no, never.*

*

Briefly, our conversation veers from the topic of Dad. You want to know why everyone was always asking you out. Why men lurked in the shadows waiting for you to dump your boyfriend, or looked you up in the phonebook, or recognized you after years and years. It doesn't make sense given how reclusive you were and still are. You're sure you could have spent your whole life alone and been happy.

I didn't say it, but I'll say it now: it's because you are beautiful. Duh.

1981

A week after she dumps Jimmy, the phone rings in Ellen's apartment on Marquam Hill.

"How'd you get this number?" she asks Bob.

"From Jimmy."

"You heard we broke up and the first thing you did was ask for my number?"

"The guy had it up on his fridge. Any jazz guitarist in Portland could have called you."

She wraps the coiled phone cord around her wrist. "I guess I'm lucky it was you."

On their first date, he sits with his back to the restaurant's brick wall and tells her he moved to Boston after high school but came back to Portland to bear witness to his parents' brutal divorce, his siblings' ensuing crises. Lately he's been living with his best friend's mom. He works in a guitar shop in Tigard and, as it happens, has no bank account, carries all his cash in a leather briefcase with a long, frayed shoulder strap.

She nods and smiles. She knows how to open a bank account; she can show him. They grew up in the same neighborhood, bought magazines from the same spinning racks at Fred Meyer in Gladstone. Ellen remembers one of his sisters from dance team, pretty and popular, seemingly sure to make something of herself. Has she?

"Not quite," Bob says.

Did he notice Ellen in high school? Yes. Did she notice him? "Of course," she lies.

She tells him she's divorced, the turning point of dates past. He doesn't care. Or he cares deeply and is unafraid. She is vehement in her anti-Mormonism. She is furious with her mother and will be for years. Now it's his turn to nod along, accidentally forming a grudge that will outlast hers.

On her nights off he comes to her apartment. Their legs overlap on a thrift store couch as they drink wine and listen to Pat Metheny records. They have sex early and often and both feel guilty about it. The guilt is something she would like to fling into the ocean but can't. The guilt has been the governing force of her life; she's not ready to give it up.

Late that summer, tanned and too thin, they are walking along the Clackamas River when he takes her hand and asks her to cancel the Europe trip she has been planning, and saving for, all year. She's going with her coworker Joy and her sister-in-law Lucy. They'll be gone four months.

Four months is longer than they've been together and also too long to live without her. They have discussed logistics; she's given him the addresses of post offices and embassies in the cities she'll be traveling through. He can write and she will write, and if they're still in love after four months, she has promised they can try to stay in love forever. No ring this time. Not enough cash in the briefcase—and anyway, she's worn too many rings.

One more thing: could she change her plans? She has borrowed money from Joy for plane tickets; she has taken an unpaid leave from work, baffling her boss, who assumed pregnancy. But can't she change her mind? He's in love with her.

Like Sam and Casey and William, he's in love with her.

<<<<>>>>

I had just graduated from college. You and I drank a bottle of wine each at the lodge in Yachats. From the window seat we could see the ocean consuming the tall, jagged rocks that bordered the hotel. Dutifully, you kept an eye on the family venturing too close to the incoming tide. "That's not a great idea," you said to me. "People need to be careful."

By now I knew their names: William. Casey. Sam. The sun went down and we searched for them on Facebook, finding only Casey, his face still gaunt, smile crooked, arm around an alpaca somewhere above tree line. In fairness, I showed you the profile pictures of boys for whom I'd fallen in high school. I told you about the senior who locked eyes with me at the homecoming dance my freshman year. He messaged me that same night: *I feel like I already know you.* He and I were on the bridge at George Rogers Park when I scrambled onto the railing and walked it like a tightrope, forcing him to grab my hand.

Did I tell you about meeting Dan? He and I were engaged before I turned twenty. I'm guessing I kept those memories, fresh, to myself.

Sophomore year of high school I applied for the summer creative writing program at Columbia, knowing we couldn't afford it and, out of self-preservation, assuring you I wouldn't get in. I showed my acceptance letter to Bob while he was stirring a pot of marinara sauce. He said, "Oh my god," with the pride of a father and despair of a man about to charge five thousand dollars to a credit card. I had applied to the beginners' workshop but the instructors moved me into the advanced workshop before I showed up. I went because I wanted to see New York and because I wanted someone to tell me I could write.

Imagine me: leather flip flops, tangled hair down my back, petrified of getting lost on the subway. Imagine Dan: white sneakers his mother picked out, book of poems, smacking a pack of Lucky Strikes against his palm. He was smarter than me. He was nearly as sullen; he moved in slow motion through a smog of suburban cynicism, but was kind, genuinely kind, to everyone he met. It was maddening and thrilling, how dismissive he was of everything I held dear—including God, my childhood romances, the sharpness of my hipbones. He kept trying to kiss me and I kept pushing him away for reasons I didn't understand.

I told him I was saving myself for marriage, which, after everything else I'd told him, was either a bad lie or a good joke.

When we said goodbye that summer, at the subway entrance on 116th Street, I felt desperate to get back to my friends, to bonfires and barbecues, boys I knew who worked at carwashes and drove crumbling Datsuns to the coast. And then I was as far from Dan as I could get, letting the Pacific soak my rolled-up jeans, and I knew I had made a mistake. My feelings for him were not fictional or willed into existence. They were real, which meant there was doubt and disappointment, terror mixed in with love. It was clear to me, suddenly, that I would marry Dan Schillinger or I would marry no one.

I was newly sixteen. Toward the end of my twenties, friends began to ask with increasing frequency: how did you *know*? I resented the question, the way Christians dislike being asked to drudge up proof of God. I didn't know, I only wanted. I wanted without ambivalence or reservation. Was it the same unadulterated want that led you to accept all those marriage proposals? Was I lucky that Dan turned out to be who he is?

Dan proposed to me after we'd both graduated from college and moved into the apartment on Lovejoy Street. He proposed, but I was unsurprised. I was the one who, during the last few months we were both high school students on opposite coasts, said into the phone, "The problem is I'm in love with you," when we hadn't been discussing love or problems. Freshman year, Dan considered transferring from Carleton College in Minnesota to Reed College, three miles from my apartment, and his dad told him he should not move to Portland for a girl unless there was at least a fifty percent chance he would eventually marry me.

Dan and I were piled on top of each other in the yellow armchair I'd taken from your living room. We were drinking Coronas from a six-pack I'd asked Andy to buy me from the Plaid Pantry. "Isn't that absurd?" Dan said. "What does marriage have to do with anything? I'm probably not going to marry you."

I laughed at him. I thought it was endearing he didn't already know.

I want to credit you, somehow. As if you getting it wrong so many times cosmically enabled me to get it right. As if a girl inherits her mother's mistakes, the resulting aversions and life lessons. What I can say more precisely is that you always took dead-seriously the idea of love. Your belief in marriage was braided with your belief in God. Because my romance with Dan was the nail in the coffin of my faith, I have always considered my marriage a rejection of God, a "fuck you" to my churchy childhood.

Now, I think it was both. I married an atheist Jew from Westchester, sure. But my mother had taught me reverence. You taught me prayers and oaths. As a teenager, I loved my boy-friend with a religious fervor.

As an adult, I would sooner die than give that up.

We get vaccinated at a concert hall deep in the half rural suburbs of Connecticut. Wes wants to know what a concert is, and then he wants to know why he's never been to one. He watches the needle penetrate my arm. His eyes are frantic above his cloth mask. "Does it hurt?" he asks. I shake my head and let him have the sticker.

One week later we leave on the Masterpiece Road Trip. It's called the Masterpiece Road Trip after the music video for Wes's favorite song, "Masterpiece" by Big Thief. The video, filmed and uploaded to YouTube before the band got big, includes footage of Adrianne Lenker and her three bandmates on tour. They mess with saltshakers at roadside diners, rehearse in the back of a 1980s camper van, select snacks from gas stations. We play the song in the car as we merge onto the highway and leave Connecticut behind. Over the course of the summer we'll play the song approximately two hundred times. Eventually, I will understand it as a song about a mother and a daughter.

We sleep in whatever pet-friendly rentals we're able to book last minute. A farmhouse in central Pennsylvania. A double-wide outside Iowa City whose every surface is smothered in throw pillows. Motels with parking lot swimming pools. Airbnbs that smell like cats. In Ohio we revisit the town where Dan had his first teaching job out of grad school—where I bit moons into my arms when Wes wouldn't sleep and, after seven winters in Toronto, spent as much time outside as I could, Wes in his stroller or strapped to my chest. You were comfortable here, I remember, walking into Walmart and marveling, "I haven't seen this much Velveeta in one place since the seventies."

Ashland, Ohio is a backdrop now. Static and strangely charmless. The little white house with the screen door falling from its hinges looks like any house I've never lived in. It's pouring rain and still we drive to the nature preserve to walk the three-mile loop we walked every weekend in 2017. Wes splashes in puddles and touches frogs with the pad of his index finger. I feel nothing except damp in jeans I have no way of washing, until the trail approaches the edge of the woods and the dog remembers where we are.

Hank bolts ahead, cutting through the long grass, leaping over cattails, splashing into the pond. He stands belly-deep in green water and grins at me, the map of my life carved into his mind.

*

Our Airbnb outside Chicago features exposed scalding pipes and the detritus of a drug-fueled party. Wes races into the bathroom while the dog noses the broken furniture. Dan fiddles with the car key in his hand. There's a high-pitched, elongated note: a teakettle in acute distress. I lurch into the bathroom to find a clip-on bidet spraying Wes in the face. The floor is flooded.

"Sprinkler!" Wes gasps. "I was trying to flush and—sprinkler!"

Dan reaches around me and shuts off the water. Laugh-crying, we fail to mop up the mess with the rental's only towel. We bail. At an expensive hotel on the loop, a concierge brings Hank his own bed and branded bowls. Wes falls hard for Millennium Park, the L, the view of downtown from the fifteenth floor. He sleeps soundly on an air mattress. He sleeps soundly every night.

*

In Omaha we lose him. He disappears in the strange house we've rented, in a strange town, at three in the afternoon. Searching for him, all thoughts and fears and expectations for my life are suspended. Then I find him in an overlooked room, hiding beneath a tangle of blankets, ignoring the desperation with which I've been calling his name. I scream until his chin wobbles and his eyes spill over. My rage is bottomless, terrifying, the kind of thing women are well-trained to hide. I want to say my rage has only ever had two victims: my son and myself.

You would know if that's true.

*

The last time we were in Denver was for our friend Jeremy's funeral. The apartment we rented, in which I got pregnant for the first time, had been covered in internet aphorisms scrawled on scraps of paper: *Smile Every Day. Life Works When You Do.* I went back to Toronto and miscarried, but there remains, in my mind, a connection between our dead friend and our living son. This is not what I say to Jeremy's mother when we pull into her driveway and let our dog loose in her backyard. Or when she presents Wes with a container of wooden blocks and he wants to know, "Who drew on this triangle? Who put glue on these squares?"

At a playground near her house, Phillipa asks me if Wes is in school. I refer, obliquely, to the series of events leading to now. Frowning, she tells me Wes is a four-year-old boy: active and defiant. Fast and feral and affectionate. I believe her. I remember Jeremy in college, that weirdo. Skinning roadkill on

123

the roof. Sleeping curled into a red armchair he'd salvaged from a dumpster and called "the womb." Smiling when his mom's number lit up his phone.

*

We are in Grand Junction, the only Airbnb for which we paid too much on purpose. The couches are brown leather, the linens white, the kitchen counters marbled. A heavy telescope points toward the glass doors facing the mesa and is quickly toppled by Wes, though I've begged him to be careful. After his bath, he springs as he springs every night from the water and tears down the hall shouting nonsense—all his "big noises"—until he slips and falls. Not bruised, not yet. Not cracked open or concussed or bleeding this time. Bone-tired is when he loses control, refusing his resting heart rate. I want to know why he is never subdued, never heavy-limbed. Why he doesn't try harder to avoid my anger. These questions bleed into those I was only ever forced to ask: why won't he fill a peg board, stack cups, drizzle glue on paper? Why won't he use more words, spoons, crayons, colors, metaphors? Even as a baby his gestures were erratic, never precise. Too often I compared him to my friends' infants, their pudgy index fingers extended toward lightbulbs.

I tell him it's bedtime and he doesn't listen; he echoes what I've said and dissolves into laughter. I present him with pajamas and he screams in my face. Equally animal, I wrestle him to the floor and scream back. This ends the only way it can, with Wes clinging to Dan, me jealous and ashamed.

Later, Dan and I sit on the patio and stare at the sun bleeding into the mesa, headlights caressing the canyon. I cry and apologize.

Dan drove the family west of Denver, supposedly a necessity for my happiness, and no one will stop crying. I worry about

Wes's development, and that all our ideas are bad. I worry Dan won't forgive my worry or my violent, juvenile expression of it.

Where the concrete meets the sand, the dog lies panting. My love for the dog is so easy.

"You don't need to apologize to me," Dan says. "You need to go easier on Wes…and on yourself."

*

Maybe I am intentionally overloading my son with memories to dilute those of my anger. Short on storage space, he will forget me smacking door frames, hissing time-outs through my teeth, tightening my grip on his shoulders. Forget, for good measure, his preschool teachers' names and the wobbly shape of their hysteria. Instead, he will remember jumping from a boat ramp into Utah's Green River. Or peeing in a wooden outhouse perched on the dizzying edge of a rocky red canyon. The wild burros loitering outside a sun-washed gas station in Beatty, Nevada. The bag of chocolate donuts within reach of his car seat.

But I know that's not how memory works, and so I pray he remembers all of it.

*

On my hard drive is a home video from the early nineties, which a friend digitized for me in high school. You were filming a river rushing through a wooded valley, having driven from Portland to Yellowstone alone with three children in a sky-blue Plymouth Voyager.

"Emily!" your voice rises above the river's roar. "You *promised* me you wouldn't whine!"

I am three, clinging to your leg off-camera. "Yes," I acknowledge, before whining in shrill denial, "No! I didn't!"

You hate this video. The sharpness of your voice, impatience creeping toward rage. Your foolish invocation of a promise made by a toddler.

I love this video. My mother in her early thirties, driven to the brink by her own offspring and proclivity for road trips, wanting only to document some river. I could not love her more.

I think of you as our car cuts across Utah on I-15. That road
trip with your three small children was the only time you
ever went back to Rexburg. LaVerne was living there. In my
three-year-old way, I asked your mom why she emerged from
her room each morning fully dressed, never lounging in pajamas. She asked me if I knew about modesty. (I didn't.) I have
never wondered why Bob stayed home, but I have wondered
why you went at all.

At sixteen, I stood at the edge of the Oregon City bluff
above the paper factory sprawling into the river and hoped I
would eventually go a year without seeing that view. In fact,
something like fifteen years passed before I walked that path
again, and when I did it was with Wes scrambling over the
rocks, yelling about boats and bridges. Did you drive your kids
across Idaho so that the breathing facts of your adulthood would
eclipse your youth? Did it work?

Something I believe, vainly, about westerners is we travel for
a reason. It's only back East that people board planes just to lan-
guish on strange sands, shop for scarves in foreign cities. In Oregon, didn't we grow up with a covered-wagon conviction that
every trip has a purpose—existential, if not practical? You used
to drive me to the mountains and the coast in order to tell me
what your life had been like, and probably to find out about

mine. Did it work? I used to read aloud the sentiments scrawled in guestbooks: *thank you Jesus. Thank you Earth Mother. Thank you Melissa and Dave for sharing your beautiful home.* I added my own entries, spoof poems about ocean waves heaving like breasts in a corset, trying to make you laugh until you cried.

In my twenties, when I lived in Canada, people would ask about my family. I would say my mother was never particularly impressed with or disappointed in me. This was a brag. What I meant was you've accepted me as I was in every moment of my life.

Driving to Deep Springs, I know what I'm asking of the desert: make Wes make sense to me. Make my flaws as a mother recede into the Western landscape. Deliver us from the social norms of New England, the absurd rigor of ivy league preschool, the pandemic. Save me from making the same mistakes over and over.

Will it work?

In September of 1981, never having crossed east of Chicago, you flew to Europe with your coworker Joy and your sister-in-law, James's wife Lucy. Over three months, weighed down by a heavy pack, its external frame bruising your hips, you took trains and occasionally hitchhiked across England, Scotland, France, Italy, Germany, the Netherlands, Switzerland, and Austria. Right now I am reading your diary from that fall. It's difficult. I mean it's literally difficult to read: in places the ink has bled. On some pages you wrote in pencil, which has now almost completely rubbed away. On other pages you worried about running out of space and so crammed your words together. I find myself annoyed with your lack of foresight, your belief you were writing only for yourself in the year 1981.

You have always been more interested in this part of your life than I am—both as your daughter and as a writer. In our interviews, you were excited to tell me about the trip and probably disappointed I didn't ask more questions. The thing is, backpacking around Europe in your twenties is ordinary. Everyone backpacks around Europe; no one counts wild horses from a two-seat Cessna or claws her own way out of the Mormon church at age twenty-one.

After a gloomy week in the UK, you wrote, *The weather today was just what this kid needed!* Your corniness embarrasses me, as it still sometimes does. But suddenly I think I understand why your Europe trip stands out as a defining event of your life. You may have felt brave and independent unrolling your sleeping bag across the pitted ground of a Scottish cow pasture— you were!—but the fall of 1981 was also the only time in your life you got to be a kid.

You wrote, *I feel like I am living in a fantasy.* You also wrote, *I feel like I am home.* From a youth hostel in London you wrote, unselfconsciously, *Look out world, here I come!* After a twenty-mile hike in Scotland, your cursive collapsing, you were *enchanted again + again + again.* You and Joy and Lucy flirted with new boys each night. In a pub, two young men explained the mechanics of a British "smooch": similar to a bear hug. You and Joy *couldn't help showing them what an American smooch was!* In the margins you let lines of James Taylor, Neil Young, and Joni Mitchell bleed into your own bad poetry. During the day you smoked yourself sick and at night drank enough beer to sleep soundly in youth hostels, missions, B&Bs, train cars. (*Guinness is great!*) In Florence, a man asked what you were going to do with your life. You told him, *I had a clearer picture of it all at fourteen than I do at twenty-three.*

You were lovesick. *I can't help but be a little skeptical that he really knows he wants to spend his entire life with me. I, for one, know the possibility that he may swallow those words.* You missed Bob more than you thought you would. You loved him more than you knew you did. You were done wasting your time on fruitless relationships. In Rome, you wrote: *He's different and complex—I know that. He's also simple and easy—but he doesn't know that.*

You were nearly as preoccupied by God, pulling open the ancient doors of every church you found and sliding into a pew. Stained glass and vaulted ceilings made you cry. On mountaintops in Switzerland or skinny-dipping in the Mediterranean you wanted *to feel close to this particular God in this particular form all the time.* In Rome you climbed the Scala Sancta, all twenty-eight steps on your knees and *felt significant.* You were going to *need more of that now.* You wanted to *hang onto that feeling* the rest of your life.

Jesus Christ, you were hard on yourself. Every argument with Joy or missed train was your fault. When Lucy went missing for several days in late October only to pick up the phone in Portland when you called your brother collect, her crushing homesickness was your fault too. You were mad at yourself for smoking. Mad at yourself for eating meat pies and pastries. You thought you should be better at guitar or writing or sketching— some kind of art. You made lists of things to work on: weight. Health. Treating everyone you met with compassion. Prayer. Worship. Political activism: you gave yourself strict orders to *find a cause and join it!*

From ten thousand feet in the Swiss alps, you wrote William a letter. You informed him you were down to 120 from the *144 pounds he knew.* You were still struggling to quit your vices—*such as lying and smoking.* Why was he still on your mind three years later? *You were my first husband,* you explained, *and I take that very seriously.* Reading this letter my heart starts to race, as if I'm listening to you leave an unhinged voicemail on his machine. Desperately I want to stop you from sending it—though I know you won't, because you didn't. Forty years later, the letter is here with me.

Over and over you write that *you want to know what life has in store for you.* I don't want to be responsible for the answer. The answer is not that you married Bob Adrian, had three children, and worked at OHSU well into your sixties. That when your dad died in 1983 you cut off all your hair and drove your brother's Jeep Wagoneer back to the farmhouse in Ontario. That your teenage sister moved in with you and moved out when she got pregnant. That you opened a guitar shop with Bob, or got thyroid cancer as a result of long-ago radiation exposure (your earliest memory is of sitting on a porch in Arizona, the desert sky pulsating orange). The answer is not that you cried in Canada as your mother began to die in Texas, or that you flew from Toronto to Dallas to be with her in the end. That you ran 10ks and half marathons, went to Europe twice more: once with Bob when you turned forty and again with me, your sister, and her daughter a few years after that. The answer is not the number of houses you've lived in (could you even count?) or the tally of grandchildren, grand-pets, grand-emergencies. Not the pandemic that filled your ICU, the wildfires that made your eyes water and burn, the ice storms that left you without power for weeks. No one's death is the answer: not your dad's, mom's, or Earl's. Not Earl's daughter found beneath the 405 bridge.

I want to point out that you never stopped asking this question. That your curiosity is your defining trait.

On November 24, 198_, you returned to Paris at the tail end of your trip. Waiting for you at the American embassy was a letter from Bob. Due to a clerical error at some post office between Paris and Portland, this was the first you'd heard from him in four months. You sat on the marbled floor and cried, the letter shaking in your hand. You imagined returning to France with him someday. You saw yourself on the beach in a bikini and sundress, Bob playing guitar in the sand. But, you cautioned yourself, it would be a while before you could save up for another Europe trip. In the meantime, the two of you could drive cross-country and see America. Maybe in the summer of 1982?

This won't happen. You are six months from getting pregnant with your first son.

Wes is in his car seat bellowing "Masterpiece," his ukulele hopelessly out of tune and, by this point, missing a string. I twist against my seat belt to lock eyes with him and shout the chorus: *You saw the masterpiece! She looks a lot like you!* Singing with him like this is, objectively, almost identical to my most shameful moments, the two of us screaming at each other. Is this all he wants? To make noise with me? Because I can do that. His cheeks dimple and flush with happiness, and I understand he is extraordinary.

We speed through the desert outside of Las Vegas, past dense tumbleweeds and abandoned motorcycles. That we drove all this way with our dog in the trunk seems impossible. That we can ever drive home, equally so.

Having built in time for an emergency that never happened, we are left with twenty-four hours to kill in Vegas. I try to convince Dan to take us to Deep Springs a day early, but after all the last-minute changes we've inflicted on everyone there, he refuses. Wes wants to see the city and so, after waking up in an airport La Quinta, we crawl through traffic on the strip. At no point does Wes accept the shaggy palm trees or tiered hotels or groups of bachelorettes pulling down their masks for 10 a.m. jello shots as "the city." We end up in a drive-through taqueria by the hotel. We end up in the pool, shivering among dead wasps and oleander leaves.

Dan says, "I bet we're not the first family to serve time in this pool before heading to Deep Springs." He comforts me by turning our boredom, our apprehension, into a tradition.

*

On a night in late November, 1981, you got off a plane at PDX in the same jeans you'd been wearing since August, head-rest-flattened hair and bags beneath your eyes. Joy had complained the entire time the plane was in the air and you—who had showered with her in youth hostels, referred to her as your "female soulmate" on more than one page—were ready to never see her again. You owed her three hundred dollars.

At the gate, leaning against a gray column, was Bob. You saw him in his corduroy pants and thought, *my husband.* You had married him somewhere over the Atlantic and were going home with him now. If you ever filled another diary, I never found it. I found scraps sometimes. A page on which you'd written, *Emily is such a volatile child,* causing me, age nine, to burst into tears. A list of Spanish verbs plus the name of your firstborn and an arrow pointing to GOD. Not once did I recognize your handwriting in a drawer and think to allow you privacy—a crime for which I'm certain you paid me back, no matter what you say.

The airport reunion is the point at which I meant to stop writing about you. For as long as I can remember, I've considered this scene the beginning of you as I know you—of your life as my mother. But did it feel like a beginning to you?

On May 12, 2021, we drive into Deep Springs Valley, down gravel-strewn switchbacks hugging treeless mountains. Where Route

168 straightens and slopes we can see the irrigated green of the college and an outpost of two sheds and a few flat ranch houses. We will live here. A sign on the gate outside Henderson Station says:

NO TRESPASSING
NO FUEL   NO PHONE
FOR EMERGENCY HELP
PLEASE GO TO
DEEP SPRINGS COLLEGE
←
1 MILE

The sign is receding into the sage tangled with the chainlink fence, and I wonder why it's needed.

In the living room is a fireplace we will never use. The mantel is fused to the brick with horseshoes and cluttered with dried desert flowers, clouded glass jars, rabbit skulls, a cheaply framed Picasso print, and a large clock stuck at 9:43. On the wall beside a couch that might be older than me is a poster of Earth labeled THE PLANET EARTH. The floors will soon be covered in the bits of hay that cling to the dog's fur before he comes inside and shakes. At night, deer mice will move freely about the house, shitting on kitchen counters and chewing holes in avocado peels. As the weather warms, then burns, ants will crawl on every surface of the bathroom. Spiders will spin webs in the corners of the ceiling and we will squint at their plump abdomens, hoping they're not venomous. In the yard, jackrabbits will learn Hank is no coyote, no threat.

The mountains to the east are gold; to the west they're the darkest blue. I will memorize their peaks as I wash dishes or try to write.

Tonight, Wes falls asleep easily, wrapped in his blankets from home. Dan and I sit facing each other on the couch, nursing Coronas and exhilaration. Is this a beginning? I want this to be the middle, the marrow of my life. At age thirty-one my only assets are a large dog, a car I'm still paying for, a willingness to pack it up and leave. You did this to me. I'm trying to understand how.

1983

From 99-West she takes a sharp right and pulls into a spot outside Tigard Music, between Les Schwab and Fred Meyer. The air through her Toyota's cracked window smells like damp moss and movie theater popcorn. It's raining but will be summer soon. She focuses on the white stucco storefront, waiting for Bob to push through the door so she can pull Andy from his car seat, complete the handoff, and make it to the hospital in time for her shift.

Toward the end of her pregnancy, late last year, she became paranoid about chemicals. At work she mixed chemotherapy for her patients and at night she dreamed of a baby with the wrong number of arms, a scrambled face. In her third trimester she quit her job, promising to return six weeks after giving birth. Between quitting and going into labor, she worked as a home health aide for a boy who had been brain-injured in a train crash.

When Andy was born—four limbs, face conventionally rumpled—she brought him home to their one-bedroom house and half cradled him while she learned to breastfeed from a library book. When things got bad, when the night yawned as infinite as the baby's screams, Ellen fixated on the front door with its frosted glass and willed LaVerne to walk through it. The fantasy verged on hallucination: LaVerne-but-not-LaVerne moving with purpose, plucking the infant from her daughter's

137

arms and vanishing with him into safe, inscrutable darkness. In reality, she knew, her mother would sit on the couch. Request a pop. Maybe hold Andy while Ellen took a shower.

That didn't happen, either.

Her first night back at work, she was briefly elated to be un-tethered from the baby, thrilled to be alone behind the steering wheel—until her eyelids grew heavy at a stoplight and she realized it was hopeless. She would never not be tired. That spring, the hospital had her working three weeks on nightshift followed by a week on days. This cycle repeated for half a year until she shut herself inside her boss's office and sobbed. Her schedule is better now. Three p.m. to 11 p.m., four days a week. She's curious about what it would be like to have another baby. Soon her curiosity will morph into insistence.

Finally Bob appears, guitar case bumping against his hip as he walks. He slides a hand between her unzipped fleece and sea foam green scrubs, touching her waist as they kiss. Then he pulls Andy, large-headed and lightly drooling, from the back. "Hello," he says, as if meeting his baby for the first time. "Ready to go home and take a very long nap?"

"Good luck with that," says Ellen. Awaiting Bob at the house is a sink full of dishes, several glass bottles of expressed breastmilk, and the large beautiful dog Bob brought home from the pound two Sundays ago when he felt his life lacked mo-mentum. The dog is always bouncing and panting with needs unmet and unmeetable. When a door opens, he runs through it and does not willingly return.

The large beautiful dog is an insurance plan. When every-thing becomes too much, they will have something to give away.

*

The closer I get to the end of this book, the more I resist fleshing out scenes from your life with fabricated details—a process that felt crucial fifty pages ago. I want to be done guessing at the song crackling through the radio, the errant thought drifting through your head.

I'm comfortable with the smell of moss and popcorn, Dad's guitar case, your hospital scrubs. I actually remember those things; it's safe to assume you do too. But pretending to remember what you don't, and couldn't possibly, has begun to feel like a rehearsal for something I don't want to happen.

Traditionally, a writer waits for her mother to die before eulogizing her in a memoir.

If I genuinely believed in your death—as a possibility, let alone a foregone conclusion—I would not write this at all.

*

On our fourth day in Deep Springs the water pump breaks. Two students with toolbelts tied to their Carhartts drive an unregistered pickup truck out to Henderson Station to take a look. From the yard we watch the truck bounce across the valley, trailed by small sand storms. The students' afternoon of laboring in the sun is unsuccessful and the ranch manager tells us a crew will have to be called in from Bishop. Forty miles away, over a steep mountain pass, Bishop is the nearest town. We might be without water for a week. To tide us over, students bring us five-gallon jugs from the barn. I can almost but not quite lift a full jug toward the toilet tank without sloshing water all over the bathroom's peeling linoleum.

After two days of chasing Wes across the desert, I smell pretty bad. It's a quick initiation into smelling bad, into lifting things that are slightly too heavy. My hair turns dry and blonde.

My lips taste like blood and salt. In the valley, reality is quick to eclipse fantasy, and no one comes to Deep Springs without a fantasy. Students arrive from the suburbs of Los Angeles or the cities of the Northeast believing their Deep Springs selves will be strong enough to castrate a calf. Powerful enough to hire (and fire) their own professors. Focused enough to read Shakespeare without checking their phones—which won't pick up a signal anyway. They've agreed to spend two years isolated in the desert, three hours past the sprawl of Vegas and the brothels of western Nevada. There are no 7-Elevens or gas stations. No restaurants or coffee shops. Nowhere to flash a fake ID, even if the students permitted themselves to drink.

Faculty are also burdened by fantasy. Over mezcal margaritas, the dean tells Dan and me that new hires are often freshly divorced or widowed—drawn to the idea of heading west. I joke that Deep Springs should sign a recruitment deal with a lawyer specializing in academic divorces. She laughs and I feel my sunburned cheeks get redder; it's been years since I had a drink with a friend.

Wes hits it off with a little girl his age, the daughter of a faculty couple, whom he chases past the boundaries of the college and into the desert. I watch him like a hawk for signs of social failure, for the deficiencies his preschool teachers harped on. It's true that Wes sometimes flings sand at his friend—and she, yelping in delight, tackles him to the ground. It's true he likes to throw back his torso and scream nonsense at the sky—and his friend grabs his hands and echoes him.

At Deep Springs, Wes swims unassisted for the first time, kicking in the weedy, dreamy reservoir. He discovers lizards, coyotes, cacti, and is with us when we spot the bobcat creeping along the dry creek bed. Every day he makes us promise we're going to "Big Dinner," the communal meal at which he'll run from table to table, asking everyone, "What's your name?" He knows their names; he memorized thirty names on our first night and now wants his knowledge confirmed, celebrated. No one seems to mind.

He spends hours in the main building strumming dusty guitars with busted strings, banging on a piano, singing songs by Patty Griffin or Adrianne Lenker. He is, at every moment, alert to the signs of forthcoming adventure, rooting for deviance from anything routine. And he remains so strange. He asks the same questions over and over. He sometimes refers to our family as "we three friends." He says things that don't quite make sense: "Does Iowa have an upstairs?" "Are you still a grown-up?" When overwhelmed, he yawns repeatedly, like a dog at the vet. He remains graceless with a fork and spoon. On a cold morning in May, I give him paper and markers and urge him to copy my purple W. His face falls. He wraps his arms around himself.

"Like at school?" he asks.

Each week in the valley lasts a year. I need you here, I realize. I need to show you where I am.

One day, when this is all over, you will tell me you miss our interviews. I'll be surprised, because I never thought of the interviews as something I did for you, but a practice to which I subjected you—for my *art*. What you're really saying is you miss my attention—and I will feel vaguely aggrieved, as I often do when someone explicitly needs me. Friends I haven't texted back. Wes who has been left to bumble around the living room. Even Dan, watching me from across the bedroom. I think I am a cold person, except for when I choose not to be. That I sometimes choose warmth does not make me less fundamentally cold.

Too often, I have ignored you. On long drives and walks in the woods. During silent afternoons in some shabby apartment for which I pay too much rent. A dog's leash in my hand or a baby asleep in my arms. I know that.

I dare you to need nothing from me, to be my mother forever.

*

We wait for you in the yard, our eyes fixed on the malt-colored mountains from which you will, we hope, descend in a rental car. We can't call you, because your phone would have lost service after your last chance to stop for gas in Beatty. Wes is heavy in my arms. We're surrounded by faded Fisher-Price toys we salvaged from a garage behind the house. A car flies by at ninety miles per hour—not you. Improbably, a red van cruises close behind. We have often spent hours in this yard without seeing a car. "Not her," I say again.

"There she is." Wes points at a white sedan creeping down the shoulderless switchbacks in the distance. "Could be," I caution him—but he's right. You wave at us through the dusty windshield, profoundly unfazed by your surroundings. Wes runs to greet you in the driveway. With you he has never been shy.

Since our arrival, as I've worked on this book in the shade of cottonwoods or a cobwebbed corner of the library, I've wondered if a younger version of yourself would have thrived at Deep Springs. If the college had admitted women in the seventies and if your parents hadn't signed over your education to the Mormon church. Because I can see you here, lean and surefooted, more attentive to hygiene than some, slinging your leg over a horse, reading Plato on the roof of the dorm, pulling tuna casserole for thirty from an industrial oven. In my mind, you are open to both the scope of the project and its tinge of silliness. Both overwhelmed and oppressed by the beauty of the desert.

You sleep in our bed while Dan and I excavate a metal frame from the depths of the couch. In the morning you take your coffee to the rocking chair on the patio. I follow and you say, unprompted, "I think I would have done well here."

After dinner, you sit with me in the lush grass at the center of the main circle. Wes abandons us for the rowdy tangle of nineteen-year-olds whose soccer game has degenerated into a semi-playful, semi-earnest brawl. He accosts a student named Carla—known for leaving carcasses in the bed of anyone who fails to show up to early morning slaughters, who will later repair our broken toilet and rate my latest novel three stars on Goodreads. "I got you," he shrieks, wrestling her to the ground.

"You got me? I'm dying?" She wails in agony. "Call a doctor!"

"No!" Wes convulses with laughter as Carla pretends to bleed out. When she springs back to life, he murders her again. She allows him to kill her something like thirteen times while her friends lounge in a nearby heap, idly picking hay from a dog's haunches, laughing.

For two months, no one will wonder if Wes should be evaluated. I will realize it was a mistake to take my son to the Child Study Center—just as it was a mistake for you to walk into the Mormon Temple on your wedding day. If you had listened to your instincts, instead of to the people whom you believed to be in charge, how much pain could you have spared yourself?

And if I had taken less seriously the first pediatrician to frown at my wordless two-year-old, the preschool teachers who invoked *behaviors* when they meant *transgressions*, would I have gotten here sooner? By here I mean cross-legged in the grass, in love and uncritically enthralled with who Wes is becoming.

These questions matter less, and maybe not at all, when I consider how close we came to ignoring our instincts altogether.

*

At twelve thousand feet in the Sierra Nevada, I tell you, "All I want is for someone to promise me that Wes will grow up and be okay."

"Would you believe them if they did?"

In my backpack I'm carrying sixty ounces of water, four oranges, and a family size bag of peanut M&Ms. My temples pulse with an altitude-induced ache, which you deny feeling. "Maybe? If enough people got together and signed a letter?"

"Well." You hesitate. "I promise you Wes will grow up and be himself. And that will be better than okay."

The trail ascends, and we hike past a lake shaped like a bird's talons, bordered by aspens and wildflowers. There should be more snow on the ridge than there is. A woman with a pole in each hand and a face ten or fifteen years older than yours looks at me and says, "Good for you." She has mistaken me for a surly teenager deigning to hike with my mom, or an adventurous daughter coaching my elderly mother through a steep climb. Either way, she has gotten us wrong.

After eating our snacks, we turn and head back toward the trailhead. Gently, you try to tell me that young mothers have a myopic view of the rest of their lives. Wes's childhood is temporary; parenting him will not always be so hard.

"I don't think I understand that," I say. "I don't think I understand that at all."

Driving back to the valley, we stop in Bishop for Mexican food. Neither of us has eaten in a restaurant since February 2020, but it's June 2021 and Covid cases in Inyo County have fallen near zero. Bob calls and you answer. There's a conflict with the contractor you hired to build your new house in Camas, Washington, which will have a ground floor suite for Nana to live out the remainder of her life.

Listening to your half of the strained conversation, I register how stressed you are. How heartsick to be leaving your house outside of Portland, the place you've lived the longest, alone with your husband for nearly fifteen years. Where you planted a garden and where your adult children gathered, all three of drinking age, to get inappropriately confrontational at Christmas.

On the trail you told me, "I didn't realize most of my life would be without them," *them* being your children. But your children are not exactly gone. You meant that the early years of motherhood are a temporary version of a lifelong relationship. What that relationship becomes can be unpredictable. In our case, it's the two of us eating lunch in a Mexican restaurant in Bishop, California, you speaking unselfconsciously into your phone, me hanging on every word.

I am haunted by a popular parenting book that briefly convinced me children should remain oblivious to their mothers' moods. That Wes should understand me as permanently undaunted, unerringly neutral. I believed in this standard automatically because I knew I could never live up to it. My emotions are fiery, constant, and obvious. Should Wes be sheltered from them? Was I sheltered from yours?

I don't think you hid yourself from me—but I also don't think you expected me to see you clearly. You gave me time to grow up and choose empathy, curiosity, gratitude. You didn't hold it against me when I was Wes's age and too young to believe in my mother's autonomy.

But no, I was never oblivious to your feelings. I knew what you felt. Your emotions were the weather of my life.

*

I have steered clear of my own sex life, but have not entirely avoided yours. In fairness, I will include Dan and me sprawled naked across the bed in Henderson Station, which we have finally realized is a stack of three worn-out mattresses. Through red curtains the sun seeps unabashedly, and the whole room smells of the sage we put in a jar on the dresser. Wes is napping on his air mattress in the next room. The dog dreams in the yard.

"This is the best thing we ever did," I say. Tequila on my breath, legs still shaking. I mean the road trip, the desert, our leaving. I mean that a person is most herself when doing exactly what she wants and for no other reason.

That's something you taught me.

<<<<>>>>

Our first interview began with me saying, "My goal is to write a memoir about your life instead of mine."

As in the restaurant in Richmond, 2019, you steeled yourself. "Okay."

Nervously, I added, "You'll like it. You'll like the book."

"I'm sure I will," you said. "You want me to be completely honest with you about everything you ask me?"

"Yeah," I said, as you must have known I would. "As a novelist I spend a lot of time trying to think critically about other people. Sometimes they're people who exist and sometimes they're people I make up. And I think one of the hardest types of real-life people to see fully is your own parent."

Did I rehearse this, or was I improvising? I honestly don't remember.

"I agree with that," you said.

"It's just so weird." I began to ramble. "Part of the problem is you gave birth to me. And the other part of the problem is that it's really hard to separate your parents from you. Because if you were raised by different people, you would be a different person. So it's like taking a really hard look at yourself, I guess. But I want to try to write about your life in a way that makes you realer than real."

I said I wanted to see you *fully*. I wanted to make you *realer than real.* Now I understand this project relied on an assumption—one I would never make about myself or someone my age. I assumed you were done becoming who you are. I didn't realize the map of your life would keep changing even as I tried to pin it to the wall.

If my goal was to write a memoir about your life instead of mine, haven't I failed? This is not the story you would tell anyone about yourself. Already, I'm anxious about all that's missing. Why isn't this book more about your career? Why isn't it about your improbably close relationship with your sister, whom you still see weekly? Where's Dad? Where are the years between 1981 and 2020? Where are my brothers? Where are yours?

Each of your children would write a different book about you. That I'm the only child who will write a book does not make this one authoritative. This is a book about me. I know that.

If there's a limit to my understanding of you as separate from me, there's no limit to my understanding of myself as your daughter. My life happens within yours, its weather and terrain—a truth I have never felt more acutely than out here, beneath this sky, these mountains.

You wanted to give me God and the West. I only needed one.

*

You leave the valley after a week. Wes cries but I'm fine this time, smiling in the driveway because we'll see you in July. When the term ends, we'll drive up to Portland and spend a month at the house on Troon Drive before you sell it. This month will mean more to me than I'll let on, or even realize as it's happening. After the past year, Wes will watch TV on your couch? I will swim with Kyra in the suburban pool of my youth? I'll yell at Andy for briefly losing track of Hank at the beach on my thirty-second birthday? These will be small miracles.

It will end on a Monday morning, while you and Dad are at work. The house will be a mess of my own family's making: slobbered tennis balls wedged beneath furniture, children's books strewn across the coffee table, empty applesauce pouches and swollen nighttime pull-ups shoved into the bathroom trash. As if it's the 1990s, I'll leave a note on the kitchen table.

Sorry for the mess. Thanks for everything.
Love, Em

*

Our last interview ended with me saying, "Do you have any regrets about the way you raised your kids?"

"Yes," you said. "I wish I hadn't been so involved in religion. I don't have a lot of regrets; I always had your best interest at heart. But I have regrets about the culture I immersed our family in. I wish I hadn't done that."

*

Do you know how proud I am of having rejected religion? I can't help it. My friends are writers and academics who got presents on Christmas and chocolate on Easter without a two-hour sermon, without itchy white tights or shame. They were raised by parents who could have, at any moment, recited their grade point averages and class schedules. They were offered condoms and rides to their boyfriends' houses, dinner table diatribes against the Iraq war.

At a crowded party in Toronto when I was twenty-four, I compared a postdoc's drunken earnestness to that of a youth pastor and my friend, on her third glass of red wine, leaned toward me and said, "I can't believe you ever believed in God—it seems so unlike you."

I was offended. I wanted credit for having chosen my own life. For considering and rejecting what was offered to me. At times, I have felt so proud of these choices I've wondered if I ought to give my child something to reject. But I sense the cheapness, the manipulation behind that impulse. Like a dad from the eighties extending a pack of Marlboros to his son, gambling on the kid's repulsion.

And anyway, this narrative in which I've taken so much pride seems dubious to me now. You did not *offer* me God. You believed in God. You were saved by God, and you were my mother. All you ever offered me were drives to the coast. Cans of tuna fish and Campbell's soup. Fleetwood Mac and Joni Mitchell. The assurance that "a person can survive anything for a month." When I wanted to leave high school: "Because you *can* is a good enough reason." You offered me stories about changing your mind, leaving home and a marriage and a church. You must have known who you were raising me to be.

When I was eight or nine, I asked what you would do when you got to heaven. Heaven made me nervous. I had been told there would be no hunger or boredom, and so all I could picture was the Clackamas Town Center food court. You said your plan was to fall at Jesus's feet and weep. Your answer had the quality of being meant for someone other than a child. For yourself, maybe, or for an adult eavesdropping from the next room. (God knows I have said countless things to Wes that were not really for Wes.) The falling and weeping may have been what your Women's Devotional Bible—mysterious tomb, flowered like a tampon box—advised that morning.

"What about you?" you asked.

I had, as a child, an overweight Siamese cat whom I loved

more than any creature on Earth besides you. His head smelled like maple syrup. His belly swayed when he walked. When I palmed his small skull, he purred like a motorcycle. My cat was not yet dead, but I understood he would die before me.

"I guess I'll find Petey," I said.

You told me that was a good answer.

All I ever wanted from religion was permission to love what I loved forever.

I don't blame you for falling for eternity.

Toward the end of our time at Deep Springs, Dan drives our car to the main circle for public speaking night. Our only neighbors at Henderson Station, the cook and the office manager, have done the same. I've stayed behind to put Wes to bed. After I get him down, I dump a clean load of laundry onto the kitchen table. I'm folding towels, watching the sky fade to black over the mountains, when a stranger taps at the window.

The jolt of seeing an unfamiliar face in a remote valley—when you've memorized the faces, voices, and gaits of the few dozen people who are supposed to be there—is genuinely shocking. Keep in mind that the doors don't lock. That motorists who find themselves stranded on Route 168 are often on drugs, often armed, and always panicked to find their gas tanks empty, their phones searching for service in vain. I scream, then apologize in a rush, "I'm sorry, you scared me, I'm sorry."

I open the door. A woman with a harshly shadowed face stands frowning in loose cut-offs and a stained undershirt, holding to her chest the kind of oversized teddy bear you might win at the county fair. With her is a kid, roughly fourteen. His hair is gelled.

"Fuel," the woman insists in an Eastern European accent.

The boy, who must be her son, lifts a hand and rephrases. "Do you have some fuel?"

"No," I say, thinking of the sign on the gate, whose necessity

I once questioned. They step closer to the house, and I open the door wide enough to reveal the shepherd behind me, hackles raised. "You need to keep driving for a minute until you see a turn-off for the college."

The woman crosses her arms, squishing the bear against her abdomen. "How far?"

"One or two miles." I say, and they don't appear to understand. "You need to drive there, then wait until nine before going inside the main building. That's when *the speeches* are over."

When I invoke the speeches, something like fear flashes across the boy's face. He and his mother retreat, climbing back inside a van I now realize is crammed with passengers, duffel bags, children's toys and Igloo coolers.

These are not the first people to pull into our driveway and demand help, and for a while, I forget about them. But Dan does not come home when I expect him to. Or an hour after that. In the yard, hot wind blows my T-shirt against my skin as I squint at the college in the distance. I convince myself fewer lights are on than should be on. For the first time since we arrived in the valley, I question the rationality of living out here. I almost want to blame you for the fear that grips me now. Really, I want to blame the Mormon in me who fell for this unforgiving landscape. Do I think I'm some kind of pioneer?

Dan has his phone with him, but there's no service and he's not connected to Wi-Fi. My texts bounce. I email the dean and use the intercampus phone system to call her house. No answer. I imagine worst case scenarios: the teddy bear concealed a weapon. The whole school has been held hostage. Or already murdered. I gave the killers directions, described everyone gathered in one room listening to each another wax philosophical about life in the desert. Now Wes and I are the only survivors, stranded at Henderson Station miles from the car.

Straining my eyes searching for headlights on 168 gives me a headache. The sky above me is jammed with stars. I am irrational and hysterical, already embarrassed, cursing myself. By the time Dan comes home I'm sobbing and he feels terrible. He holds me and says that next time he stays late for drinks at the lower ranch, he'll find a way to check in with me. "When we come back, we'll live on the main circle. You won't have to be alone out here."

When we come back?

We pack up the car on July 2nd. We're meeting friends in Joshua Tree, a favorite place that will suddenly strike us as crowded, built-up, slightly shrubby. More friends and family in Los Angeles and San Francisco, some of whom we haven't seen in years. After a month with you in Portland, we'll head east for another year in New Haven. This time, and without knowing what to expect, we've enrolled Wes in public school.

In this moment, my fantasy is that we'll come back. Wes will remember the valley as a place to which he returned more than once, a touchstone of his childhood, if not a long-term home. At the very least, I want him to remember this summer. I can hear him reflecting on it years from now, when he has the capacity to examine his own memories.

"What was that place?"

"It was a school," I'll say, though that won't make sense. He won't remember chalkboards or classrooms, or even the students with paperbacks of Machiavelli's *The Prince* shoved into the pockets of their overalls. He'll remember the tire swing by the dairy barn, or climbing Chocolate Mountain on his dad's shoulders. Cookies handed to him fresh from the oven. Our car bumping along roads rutted like ribs. He'll remember the reservoir, and the mile-wide lake dried to salt with quicksand at its center—how I yelped the first time my foot cracked the crust and started to sink.

Behind our house was a massive garage. Inside the garage was an old fire truck. The garage was locked but a window was broken, and Wes wanted me to push him through the jagged glass, so desperate was he to grip the fire truck's steering wheel in his hands, to see if the bell still clanged. But I said no, it wasn't safe, and he trusted me. It has not escaped my notice that something about the desert inspires my son to trust me—which is an indirect way of admitting that, out West, where my eyes register the landscape as home, I'm better at trusting myself.

Wes will remember that you were here. That you waited for him at the edge of the alfalfa field and opted to say nothing about the snakes we knew were lurking in the grass.

"Why did we go there?" he'll want to know.

For the same reason we went anywhere.

To find out who you were.

In March of 2022, you fly to Connecticut for Wes's fifth birth-day. I give you the manuscript before you check into your Airbnb—the same apartment you rented a year ago. As soon as Dan and I are alone, I tell him you'll stay up all night reading.

"She won't," he says. "She's tired."

But you do.

In the morning, you come over while Wes is at school, where his new teachers know all about the Masterpiece Road Trip. He has told them his own stories, in his own words. That I, as recently as last June, had doubts about Wes being okay is a little bit confounding. Wes is loud, and obsessive, and sensitive, and kind. He is—as people have described me all my life—intense. If any of us are okay, Wes is okay.

You sit on the same garage sale couch we have loaded onto U-Hauls and pushed up stairwells for the last ten years. "You still have the couch," you say. You're laughing, but I worry we will always have the couch. I pray you never look beneath the cushions.

You tell me what I got wrong: a painfully inaccurate characterization of your oldest brother James. The color of the car you rented at the Las Vegas airport. The location of the jazz club where you saw Bob for the first time since high school.

"You got my mom right," you say, looking down at your coffee. "I don't know if it's because you remember her, but you

157

got her. She's right there in the book."

We list the names we need to change, separating the living from the dead. Discussing who is most likely to have a Google alert set up for himself. Who is least likely to ever bother reading a book.

You don't say a word about the parts of your life I promised to omit and didn't. Instead, you ask me to take out roughly half of what I wrote about my dad. I want to argue, but I don't. It's the only request you've made.

"I'll think about it," you say. "I might still change my mind."

Yes, I know.

"Did I not tell you about the time he left his briefcase on the roof of the car with three thousand dollars in it? We turned onto McLoughlin and all his savings flew into the bushes."

You offer me this story as if I didn't already write the book. As if the book was not really the point—and I realize it wasn't.

You will never consider our interviews comprehensive or complete. In trying to pin you down, I have opened you up, choosing to continue a conversation—one we might never have had—forever. I still owe you a road trip from Portland to Burns, through Rexburg and Salt Lake City, to Provo and back home. I owe you motel rooms, cabins, and campfires.

I meant to reveal our relationship, with all its familiar tensions and particular intimacies, but of course I also changed it. There are new rules.

"No," I say. "Tell me now."

There are new rules—but I don't know if I trust either of us to follow them.

ACKNOWLEDGEMENTS

Thank you to Michael Wheaton for editing and publishing this book: I am so glad to know you. Thank you to my agent Susan Ginsburg for everything, always. To Rufi Thorpe, Alex Higley, and Kerry Winfrey for being generous readers of early drafts. To Elisa Gabbert for the kindest blurb. To Justin Taylor, whose memoir showed me what a memoir can do.

Thank you to Sarah Stickney for letting us come to the valley. Someday I will stop claiming I'm not going to do the things I'm going to do.

Thank you to Hank, who took care of me his whole life.

Thank you to Wes. You are seven now. I was wrong about the years before your birth being the best of my life. The moment we took you to the desert, those years in Toronto were eclipsed by everything that came next. You've now spent three summers at Deep Springs; you talk to Buckwheat and Tex in your dreams.

Thank you to Dan. I love you.

Thank you to my mom for teaching me how to escape—as many times as it takes.

ABOUT THE AUTHOR

Emily Adrian is the author of several novels. Her work has appeared in *Granta, Joyland, EPOCH, Alta Journal,* and *Los Angeles Review of Books*. Originally from Portland, Oregon, Emily lives in New Haven, Connecticut with her family.

{a}

— also from Autofocus Books —

Duplex — Mike Nagel

XO — Sara Rauch

Until It Feels Right — Emily Costa

Cleave — Holly Pelesky

Nextdoor in Colonialtown — Ryan Rivas

Too Much Tongue — Adrienne Marie Barrios & Leigh Chadwick

Picture Window — Danny Caine

the nature machine! — Tyler Gillespie

A Kind of In-Between — Aaron Burch

How to Write a Novel: An Anthology of 20 Craft Essays About Writing, None of Which Ever Mention Writing — ed. Aaron Burch

Hiraeth — Mistie Watkins

That Spell — Tate N. Oquendo

My Modest Blindness — Russell Brakefield

A Calendar Is A Snakeskin — Kristine Langley Mahler

Culdesac — Mike Nagel

Razed by TV Sets — Jason McCall

In the Away Time — Kristen E. Nelson

The Body Is A Temporary Gathering Place — Andrew Bertaina